MOEBIUS

FREDERICK LUIS ALDAMA, SERIES EDITOR

MOEBIUS

NICOLAS LABARRE

UNIVERSITY PRESS OF MISSISSIPPI / JACKSON

The University Press of Mississippi is the scholarly publishing agency of the Mississippi Institutions of Higher Learning: Alcorn State University, Delta State University, Jackson State University, Mississippi State University, Mississippi University for Women, Mississippi Valley State University, University of Mississippi, and University of Southern Mississippi.

www.upress.state.ms.us

The University Press of Mississippi is a member of the Association of University Presses.

Title page portrait by Antony Hare

Manufactured in the United States of America
∞

Library of Congress Cataloging-in-Publication Data

Names: Labarre, Nicolas, author.
Title: Moebius / Nicolas Labarre.
Description: Jackson : University Press of Mississippi, 2025. | Series: Biographix | Includes bibliographical references and index.
Identifiers: LCCN 2024036150 (print) | LCCN 2024036151 (ebook) | ISBN 9781496854971 (hardback) | ISBN 9781496854988 (trade paperback) | ISBN 9781496854995 (epub) | ISBN 9781496855008 (epub) | ISBN 9781496855015 (pdf) | ISBN 9781496854964 (pdf)
Subjects: LCSH: Moebius, 1938–2012. | Cartoonists—France—Biography. | Comic books, strips, etc.—France—History and criticism. | LCGFT: Biographies. | Comics criticism.
Classification: LCC PN6747.G5 Z74 2025 (print) | LCC PN6747.G5 (ebook) | DDC 741.5/944 [B]—dc23/eng/20240814
LC record available at https://lccn.loc.gov/2024036150
LC ebook record available at https://lccn.loc.gov/2024036151

British Library Cataloging-in-Publication Data available

CONTENTS

ACKNOWLEDGMENTS

Many people deserve heartfelt thanks for making this book possible. Frederick Luis Aldama, of course, who agreed to the idea, but also Jean-Paul Gabilliet, Daniel Pizzoli, and Christophe Quillien, whose help and support proved invaluable in carrying the project to fruition.

MOEBIUS

CHAPTER ONE

INTRODUCTION

When Jean Giraud, who signed his major works as *Gir* and *Moebius*, died in 2012, he was celebrated globally as one of the most important comics artists ever, as a defining influence on contemporary popular visual culture, and even as a transcendent artist: a genius. Along with Richard Corben and Robert Crumb, he was one of the medium's first true international superstars in the 1970s, and over forty years later, he had retained his place in the "pantheon" of comics creators (Smolderen 2000).

Since his death, several attempts have been made to capture his graphic style and to identify the formula underlying some of his most memorable images. When the independent videogame *Sable* was first presented in 2018, the *Verge* noted: "It's like a comic from Jean 'Moebius' Giraud has been brought to life in three dimensions" (Webster 2018). The game's creative developer acknowledged the influence, along with that of Studio Ghibli's luminary, Hayao Miyazaki, further noting the circularity of these sources, as Moebius's work had inspired Miyazaki's own *Nausicaä of the Valley of the Wind* (1984) (Peltz 2021; on Miyazaki and Moebius, see Valembois 2004).

Sable generates its graphics on the fly, using black outlines around and within the three-dimensional shapes of its game world. The effect approximates the look of pen and ink on paper, enclosing areas of solid colors from a palette of mauve and tan. The game further heightens the proximity with Giraud's work as Moebius through various design choices and by setting its action in a peaceful postapocalyptic desert where masked characters interact with mystical presences, rendered as smooth, animated volumes.

Sable represents one of the most sustained efforts to understand and replicate what made Giraud's comics instantly recognizable. To some extent, this is a success: playing the game, even for a few minutes, conjures a sense of familiarity, an echo of his singularity. It confirms what critic Matt Seneca vividly wrote about Giraud's design sense throughout his career: "At its core is visionary potential, the ability to make things imagined seem real" (2018). *Sable* inverts this axiom: instead of suggesting a world out of ink on paper, it cloaks a simulated three-dimensional environment in the guise of Giraud's drawing. In doing so, it celebrates the drawing style it painstakingly seeks to automate and replicate, proclaiming its ability to conjure fictional worlds into existence. The illusion of playing within a Moebius world soon dissipates, however. Automation fails, textures flicker, and the images of the game often feel accidental, devoid of an organizing principle. Most importantly perhaps, and paradoxically for a game, the automation conserves none of the playfulness contained even with the limited sample of Moebius's output which *Sable* seeks to emulate. The algorithmic stylistic features ossify, and cease to surprise, as their regularity makes them predictable.

Image generators based on deep learning, such as Midjourney or Stable Diffusion, also offer the opportunity to produce automated Moebius art. These systems draw on a vast corpus of annotated digital pictures and identify recurrences to generate specific subjects, often within specific styles. Though the efficiency of these tools tends to be overstated in reporting, they produce recognizable approximations of many artists, and even convincing imitations in some cases, like Heartfield or Mucha (Knight 2022; Heikkilä 2022). By contrast, using Moebius or Giraud as prompts generates images that have little in common with the content or style of his work.[1] A variety of factors may explain this inability, starting with the limits of the corpus used by these engines. It is also likely that these attempts will improve in the future. However, the experience demonstrates the difficulty of pinning down one Moebius style, let alone codifying it.

These unsatisfying attempts at breaking down the Moebius formula seem to confirm both his continuing relevance and his position as a transcendent artist, a genius beyond imitation. Through a critical study of Giraud's career, this book seeks to investigate the second claim.

Objectives

This work aims to provide the first book-length study in English of a comics creator whose importance spans decades and multiple media. The historiography of comics is famously lacking, with many important works, creators, and even entire periods still understudied. It is striking, however, that these gaps should include an artist whose influence on the medium was profound and immediate, making him a global role model for aspiring comics creators throughout his career: he was widely imitated while at *Métal Hurlant* and *Heavy Metal* in the 1970s, was "prominent among the spiritual fathers of the comic book rebels" in the 1990s (Wiater and Bissette 1993, 146), and again an example for the independent artists in France in the early 2000s. In the course of a career spanning more than five decades, he straddled radically different eras in the French and global comics industries, produced comic books, *bande dessinée* and manga, film and videogame art, and influenced creators as diverse as Frank Miller, Carla Speed McNeil, Katsuhiro Ōtomo, Colleen Doran, and Lewis Trondheim.

Within a mostly chronological approach, I hope to chart his career and influence and also to provide complementary frames to understand his work.[2] Thus, I will examine the industrial and cultural context in which Giraud's comics were produced. Over the course of his career, the French comics industry underwent profound transformations: in the late 1960s, with the rise of "adult comics" and the disappearance of the Catholic press (Boltanski 1975; Lesage 2019b), in the 1980s, with the shift from periodicals to albums (Lesage 2019a; 2022), then in the late 1990s, with the "new bande dessinée" and the rise of the graphic novel (Dayez 2002; Beaty 2007; Dejasse, Habrand, and Meesters 2011). This changing environment shaped Giraud's career and the specific forms of his comics, to the point where he specifically sought to regain a form of independence through self-publication in his late career. My second angle is more typical, highlighting the themes, techniques, and influence within each period, envisioning his comics at the personal rather than institutional level. Finally, I include within each chapter a close reading of a few pages of a significant work, not as illustrations, but with the conviction that these works typify and exceed the broader trends visible at the other levels. I hope that this three-tiered structure will help readers understand the ways in which Giraud's fame was achieved within specific publishing contexts and discursive communities, on the basis of distinctive and finely crafted works. The book will notably emphasize the productive tension between Giraud and Moebius in all these aspects: one name for Westerns, the other for science fiction, one name for the domestic market, another as a global brand, one name for the brush, another for the pen nib, one for the mainstream, and the other for the underground.

On Style

Understanding Giraud's career requires coming to terms with the notion of style. A certain conception of comics authorship has privileged "complete authors," who write, draw, and in certain cases control the materiality of the final book. Barbara Postema's holistic description of style seems especially applicable to such authors: "In comics, style is so pervasive that it encompasses the entire experience of the comic—the characters, the storyline, the look—often even down to the shape of the letters. Style, in effect, ceases to be style, since it is no longer a superficial matter. Style becomes the substance of comics, through which each text speaks in a voice that is completely its own. Style signifies in comics" (Postema 2013, 212).

Part of Giraud's career functioned in that mode. The books he produced in the late twentieth and early twenty-first centuries (*40 Days dans le Désert B*, *Le Major*, *Inside Moebius*, *La Faune de Mars*) were done with little to no editorial interferences and with Giraud taking charge of the entire work. Furthermore, their high prices and limited print runs signaled his willingness to remove these works from the market forces shaping regular comics, even though this move also made them specifically desirable within another market, that of collectors and speculators.

However, these late books do not sum up the entirety of Giraud's career, or even of his work in that period. As late as 2007, Giraud served as a guest artist on the eighteenth volume of XIII, a popular spy series written by Jean Van Hamme, and most of his output throughout his careers results from collaborations with writers like Jean-Michel Charlier or Alejandro Jodorowsky. From his professional debut to his death, Giraud maintained a severability between his *graphic style* and his *writing style*. As Thierry Groensteen reminds us in his online dictionary of comics terms, this distinction remains meaningful even in the case of complete authors, and it is crucial in understanding Giraud's career as a whole, encompassing his multiple collaborations as well as his independent works. Furthermore, the notion of the complete authors tends to disregard "invisible" creative functions within the comics industry—colorist, letterer, editor, designer, who frequently help these "complete" authors— but also the cultural, technological, and economic parameters shaping comics publishing, which complicate any attribution of the style of a given comic to one individual. In this book, I hope to provide an overview of Giraud's style that incorporates these parameters.

For instance, *The Airtight Garage* (1976–79), a notoriously improvised series, stemming out of pages not intended for publication, nevertheless manifests the narrative and economic constraints of comics production. The format of *Métal Hurlant*, in which the story was serialized, defines those pages, both in terms of shape (height to width ratio) and in terms of size since details and texts could not become too small or run the risk of becoming illegible. Giraud incorporated these limitations at the drafting stage, directing his process toward the potential then actualized printed product. Even though the original pages for *The Airtight Garage* vary in sizes (page 47 is 43.60×32.40 cm; page 105 is 29×22 cm), they all follow a standard 1.3:1 ratio, which made them suitable for publication without trimming and without disrupting the technical norms of production. Thierry Groensteen notes that the concept of "rests on the artist's personality, its singularity" (Groensteen 2012); however, if we agree with Postema that style is *everywhere* in comics, then style need be attributed at least in part to these norms and constraints. Andrei Molotiu's study of "cartooning" further suggests that the tools chosen by Giraud for most of his career—China ink applied with a brush, a pen, a nib, or a digital remediation of these tools—should be understood as the expression of broad constraints applying to workers in the comics industry (Molotiu 2020, 153–54). Style in comics, as in the broader art history, exists at the intersection of personal skills and choices and less easily discernable collective norms (see notably Gombrich 1968; 1996). Giraud chose to work within the formal parameters of commercially published comics, embracing these as creative constraints but constraints nevertheless.

Similar observations apply to his writing style. Plotting a Western like Blueberry implies playing by the rules of the game, in terms of setting and plot. These rules may be bent, as in the late albums, in which the heroics are forever delayed, but that deviation is framed by close adherence to the setting, the space of the genre. These limitations are not so much technical as economic and social, playing off the generic labeling chosen by cultural intermediaries (publisher, bookstores, libraries) and off the readers' expectations. Such constraints are also at play—as well as in play—in

Giraud's more personal works. Jacques Goimard, reviewing *The Airtight Garage* in *Métal Hurlant* observed that the book worked as a serial even as it professed disdain for the form: "Moebius may mock the rules of the genre, create a multiplicity of anti-events and anti-catastrophes, change the characters and the setting on a whim, ridicule ready-made lines and the summaries of previous episodes, he is nevertheless forced to move the action forward, and in spite of his reticence, he cannot help but play the game" (Reprinted in Moebius 1980, 147).

The impersonal forces and urges Goimard describes in this passage mirror the aforementioned integration of technological constraints in the shape of the pages. In both cases, Moebius could have chosen not to follow these implicit rules, but it would have been *impractical* and probably *undesirable* to do so. Giraud's public work did not break away from the complex social and aesthetic cluster that constitutes "comics."

His styles pose a final difficulty. Most of the graphic artists who commemorated his death did so not so much by imitating distinctive graphic techniques but by reusing recurrent motifs, locales, and characters from his work. His work offers not so much a fixed catalog of effects, whose sum would define Giraud or Moebius's style, but a dynamic relationship between these effects, the content of the work, and its purported uses (stand-alone illustration, book cover, ad, comics). That content—which may be his own, or conceived by others, and is in any case the result of a dialogue with collective conventions, or genres, such as science fiction or the Western—is integral to a holistic understanding of his graphic style. For instance, his two stories set in a realistic, contemporary world (*Madwoman of the Sacred Heart* and his XIII album) resemble each other more than any other book in his bibliography.

This dynamic relationship between technique and content explains the difficulty in attempting to use deep learning—mislabeled as AI—to recreate his style. The gestures, the traces of the body remain identifiable in these various configurations, but they do not ossify into staid know-how. As I hope to demonstrate in the rest of this book, Giraud's continuing relevance until the end of his career, and possible claims of having transcended the medium rest on this constant reinvention.

Author's Note

In this text, I will use *Giraud* or *Jean Giraud* to refer to the actual person. *Gir* and *Moebius* are both signatures, author's persona without independent agency, but may nevertheless be used as shorthand to refer to Giraud when working under one of these names or to refer to the author's figure in the texts.

When mentioning the works, I have used the English titles first when they exist. In other cases, I have given the French title, followed by a possible English translation.

CHAPTER TWO

Journeyman to *Pilote*

First Works

Jean Giraud was born in 1938, in Nogent-sur-Marne, in the outskirts of Paris. Raised by his grandparents during the Second World War, then by his mother in the suburbs of Paris, he started attending les Arts Appliqués, an applied art school, when he was sixteen. The school did not offer much training in illustration, much less in comics, but led to a lasting friendship with fellow student Jean-Claude Mézières (1938–2022). Mézières, the future creator of *Valérian*, shared Giraud's interest in comics and started publishing in Catholic magazines at the age of seventeen.

Giraud's first published works appeared a year later, in 1956, in a postwar comics market shaped by three decades of profound transformations. Through paper shortages and political control in occupied France, the war had put an end to what nostalgic French comics fans of the 1960s later described as a "golden age" for comics-centric children's magazines as they started massively translating modern American comic strips. While strips like *Buster Brown* or *Bringing Up Father* had been published in France since the early twentieth century, the creation of *Le Journal de Mickey* in 1934 opened the floodgate for translations of adventure, fantasy, Western, and funny animal comics in children's periodicals. Using word balloons, then a rarity in French comics (Baudry 2022), and benefitting from the graphic virtuosity of creators such as Floyd Gottfredson, Hal Foster, and Alex Raymond, these translations differed markedly from the delicately crafted but sedate illustrated stories which had been the main visual attraction of children's magazines up to that point. However, they also generated strong opposition for their violence and perceived eroticism and also by virtue of being American exports in a period of growing nationalism (Mollier 1999).

Soon after the Second World War, as the French market was rebuilding, that distrust toward popular culture, especially of American origin, led an unlikely alliance of the Communist Party and the Catholic Church to regulate comics (Crépin 1999). Both harbored concerns about US culture and the US's geopolitical reach through soft power, and both had observed firsthand the use of popular culture for propaganda purpose during the war; in fact, the Vichy régime has used a comics magazine, *Le Téméraire*, precisely for propaganda (Ory 2002).

This unlikely alliance led to the 1949 law on youthful publications, which sought to sanitize periodicals aimed at young people by forbidding any representation of monstrosities or social deviance ("light robbery, lies, thievery, idleness, cowardice, hatred, debauchery, [. . .] any crime or action liable to demoralize young people, or to foster ethnic prejudice" [my translation]). Although US comics were not explicitly mentioned in the law, they were the object of severe scrutiny, and publishers were discouraged from using this translated material. The logic and the mechanisms differed from the implementation of the Comics Code in the United States five years later—the French commission was part of the government, not an instance of self-regulation within the industry—but the 1949 law marked a similar attempt at keeping comics publications firmly within acceptable boundaries. However, unlike the backlash against comic books in the United States, the 1949 legal framework does not appear to have had a detrimental effect on the health of the French comics market.[1] By imposing protectionist measures against the importation of popular material, at a time when television was not yet a competitor for comics—only 9 percent of French households owned a television in 1959, against 85 percent in the United States—it arguably helped foster a thriving local industry in France and Belgium, freed from their most glamorous foreign competitors (Frémion 1974b; Crepin and Groensteen 1999, 217–19).

Children's magazines in the late 1950s differed from US comic books, in their content, their format, and their ideological positioning. Most of these magazines were published weekly, and while comics were their main attraction, they devoted numerous pages to other subjects, from movie stars to new technologies, often with educational purposes.[2] The comics included spanned a wide array genres and graphic styles, with short standalone stories and serialized narratives, typically in one- or two-page episodes. These magazines also existed in a variety of formats, including broadsheets (*Vaillant*, *Cœurs Vaillants*), tabloid-sized magazines (*Lisette*, *Tintin*), and pocketbook-sized black-and-white monthlies containing longer stories, often within a defined genre. A number of these popular publications were also directly affiliated with or supervised by members of the Catholic Church and devoted regular pages to religious storytelling, while *Vaillant*, one of the most successful postwar creations, was directly associated with the Communist Party.

Giraud's first year in comics illustrates this diversity and the many points of entry the field offered for newcomers. His two pages in *Far West*, issue 10, in February 1956—his first published comics—feature a humorous Western story, in this small (18.8 × 27 cm), monthly black-and-white magazine. *Far West* had started the year before, under the helm of an independent publisher and writer, Marijac, and lasted until 1957. In July of same year, Giraud was also published in *Fripounet et Marisette*, *Âmes vaillantes*, and *Cœurs Vaillants*, three magazines belonging to Catholic publisher Fleurus. Along with the Communist *Vaillant*, the Catholic girl magazine *Lisette*, and the French edition of *Tintin* magazine, the weekly *Cœurs Vaillants* was a central magazine in French-speaking comics publishing (Kohn 2018). Across its sixteen broadsheet pages, including ten in full color, it offered a mix of educational features, text stories, humorous and realistic comics, both self-contained and serialized. Like all of Giraud's initial efforts, "Blanco seigneur des prairies" (Blanco, lord of the prairie) is a Western, recounting the efforts of a young man to thwart an attack by Native Americans on a settlers' convoy.[3] Giraud's visual storytelling is ambitious, with swooping perspectives on rushing horses and panels full of figures in action, which exceed his abilities at the time (fig. 2.1). Done mostly with a nib, the actual drawings are uneven, alternating between a variety of renderings (caricatures done in outline, fully shaded figures), in barely sketched out environment. The horses are the main draw here. A notorious scourge of cartoonists, they are mostly drawn from a limited number of photo references—one is even used twice—and not devoid of anatomical mistakes. Yet, they are present in two-thirds of the panels as if to demonstrate that Giraud, at the age of eighteen, was ready to tackle the challenge. Throughout his career, Giraud never shied from acknowledging his own abilities, and this early example suggests the impulse was already present in his first year as professional.

Giraud's fascination with the American West became more concrete in mid-1956, as he departed for Mexico with his mother. This crucial excursion, during which he discovered *Mad* magazine, lost his virginity, and came to observe firsthand the America he had been drawing led to a brief hiatus in his career (Moebius 1999). He resumed work with Catholic publications from 1957 to 1959, covering the whole range of subjects expected from young cartoonists, from illustrations accompanying text features to covers and comics stories. He also continued working during his two years as a conscript from 1958 through 1960, first in Germany, then in Algeria, producing stories and illustrations for children's magazines and for *5/5*, an army publication (where he produced ninety-five pages of content, including two comics stories).[4]

Though he had been a published author for four years, in July 1960 he became an apprentice to Joseph "Jijé" Gillain, whose work Mézières and he had long admired.[5] Jijé, born in 1914 in Belgium,

Fig. 2.1. Jean Giraud, detail from "Blanco seigneur des prairies," *Cœurs Vaillants*, July 1, 1956.

had started working in comics and illustration before the Second World War and became, along with Hergé, "the other father of Franco-Belgian comics" (Delisle and Glaude 2019). He briefly took over Spirou in 1940 and helped give the character traits he has retained to this day. A year later, his comics biography of Italian priest Don Bosco sold half-a-million copies. After the war, he became a central figure for the next generation of cartoonists, including Franquin (1924–97, *Spirou*, *Gaston Lagaffe*) and Morris (1923–2001, *Lucky Luke*); according to Jean-Michel Charlier: "Since the beginning of bande dessinée, no one has trained more people than he has" (qtd. in Delisle and Glaude 2019, 165). Crucially, he also served as a bridge between American and French comics, taking over *Superman* and *Red Ryder* during the Second World War and even publishing a story in a DC romance comic book during an extended stay in the United States in 1948 and 1949. In 1954, he created a new Western series for *Le Journal de Spirou*, Jerry Spring, which offered a "great shock on realism" in francophone comics (Groth and Mézières 2004). Jerry Spring was arguably the first French Western to channel the cinematic glamour and dynamism of US strips such as *Red Ryder* or Milton Caniff's work in what Giraud later called "a kind of synthesis between classic illustration and American storytelling" (Thompson and Giraud 1987, 87).

Giraud and Mézières had already visited Jijé in late 1957, and Jijé's influence is unmistakable in Giraud's work from that point onward. His cover for *Cœurs Vaillants* in July 20, 1958—a dapper cowboy in a tight red shirt, tipping his white hat to a Native American, drawn with brush and nib—functions as a pastiche of Jerry Spring, for instance (fig. 2.2). The aesthetic filiation is especially visible in the bold brush strokes delineating the main character and the rocks in the foreground, and it extends to background details, such as the smaller rocks and the grass. Jijé had used a similar composition on the cover of *La Passe des Indiens*, published the year before, and Giraud certainly looked at that album when designing his cover. This stylistic compatibility and Giraud's already accomplished line, including his ability to draw horses, convinced Jijé to take him as an apprentice.

In later interviews, Giraud consistently thanks Jijé for providing him with the only formal graphic education he ever received, emphasizing in particular Jijé's rigor and use of photographic references (Pizzoli 1995, 89–90). His work in the early 1960s offers many instances of this training process. Some of his illustrations were touched up by Jijé, and in 1961 Giraud fully inked *La Route de Coronado*, Jerry Spring's eleventh adventure, after briefly attempting to draw it himself but failing to make the deadline for prepublication in *Le Journal de Spirou* (Bouster and Giraud 2003, 10). Subsequently, he produced stories for the promotional booklets packaged with the Bonux washing powder, *Bonux-Boy*, headed by Jijé's son.

In these early years, from 1956 to 1962, Giraud benefitted from a publishing ecosystem that offered numerous opportunities for budding illustrators, including children's magazines but also encyclopedias and advertisement. Retrospectively, it is tempting to see this period only in terms of comics work, but a significant portion of Giraud's output was in fact in spot illustrations, as was the case for many of his peers in the late 1950s. Giraud's trajectory was also typical in its combination of art school training and studio work (Kohn 2018, 122–27). By 1961, when he finished inking *La Route de Coronado*, he had overcome his most glaring technical limitations and had perfected his imitation of Jijé. In 1963, after the end of a lucrative illustration project depicting the History of Civilization

Fig. 2.2. Top, Jean Giraud, cover to *Coeurs Vaillants*, July 20, 1958; bottom, detail of the back cover to Jijé's *La Passe des Indiens*, 1957.

project, he was able to put this skill to use, when he took over a project for *Pilote* which Jijé did not have time to pursue, Blueberry.

Inventing Moebius, Looking toward the United States

Before working for *Pilote*, however, Giraud found home at a very different type of publication, the satirical magazine *Hara-Kiri*. The self-proclaimed "dumb and nasty" magazine, started in 1960, offered its readers a mix of *fumetti*, absurdist comics, and text pieces, with a surrealist streak in the work of artists like Gébé (1929–2004) and Topor (1938–97). *Hara-Kiri* was an adult magazine containing comics, as opposed to an adult comics magazine, of the kind that emerged later in the decade. In the early 1960s, it resembled *Mad* and Harvey Kurtzman's contemporary *Help!* (1961–65), two magazines that the *Hara-Kiri* authors admired. This resemblance betrayed an avowed admiration for Kurtzman and his early collaborators, notably Jack Davis and Bill Elder. *Hara-Kiri*'s publisher produced a French version of *Mad* in 1965, and in the magazine itself, George Wolinski (1934–2015) drew thinly veiled imitations of Elder's style.[6] Giraud had actually discovered the *Mad* years earlier, during his stay in Mexico, but he allowed its influence to come to the fore in *Hara-Kiri* in ways which would not have been permissible in children's magazines. As a result, the ten wryly humorous short comics stories he published there in 1963 and 1964 often look like a cross between Davis's and Elder's styles.

The first of these stories, "L'homme du XXIe siècle," (The man of the 21st century), published in May 1963, is a tongue-in-cheek satire about increasing punishments for wrong answers in quiz shows, culminating in the destruction of the earth. The satire is broad—especially compared to *Mad*'s take on similar subjects, such as the McCarthy era "What's My Shine" (Kurtzman, Davis, *Mad*, issue 17, November 1954)—but the story works, thanks to a playful use of verbal registers and of science-fiction tropes, combined with densely packed, energetic cartooning (done with brush, pen, and mechanical patterns)—"a Jack Davis type story," in Giraud's own words (Moebius 1999, 142) (fig. 2.3). Giraud had become a specialist of the realistic Western, but the *Hara-Kiri* work showcases his appetite for a quirkier take on popular genres.

Giraud did not sign these unusual stories with his own name, but borrowed the name of mathematician August Ferdinand Möbius, known for his apparently paradoxical strip. The pseudonym was a clever one—a Möbius strip has two sides yet constitutes a single, continuous surface—but Giraud stopped using it for years after leaving *Hara-Kiri*. There is no evidence that he sought to keep his work a secret, and the dual identity was clearly spelled out in *Pilote*, in March 1967 (issue 385) then in a global comics sampler the same year (Sternberg, Caen, and Lob 1967). Yet, as late as 1969, readers inquired about the identity of Moebius, when *Charlie Mensuel* republished some of these early stories, and the magazine declined to provide more information.

The publishers of *Hara-Kiri* were not the only admirers of *Mad* in the 1960s. Morris, who drew the popular cartoonish Western *Lucky Luke*, was influenced by Davis, whom he had met in New York. Similarly, Uderzo, *Astérix*'s artist, was aware of Kurtzman's work, and the background gags in crowded *Astérix* panels resemble Elder's theory of the "chicken fat" style of humor (Elder and Groth 2003, 49). However, the most influential proponent of *Mad* in France was certainly René Goscinny, the writer of *Astérix* and editor in chief of *Pilote*.

Goscinny had been a friend and colleague of Kurtzman, Davis, Elder, and Severin while struggling to make a living as a cartoonist in New York City in the early 1950s. Though he left shortly before the launch and immediate success of *Mad*, he remained close to Kurtzman afterward, and his scripts for Morris, Uderzo, and others from the late 1950s onward displayed a similar sense of humor, along with a shared appetite for meticulous preparation. With Jean-Michel Charlier, Goscinny created the weekly *Pilote* magazine in 1959. Like many other children's magazines, it contained comics but also a wide variety of educational and entertaining content,

Fig. 2.3. Jean Giraud, as Moebius, "L'Homme du XXIe siècle," *Hara-Kiri*, issue 28, 1963.

from photo-film adaptations to illustrated spreads on the latest industrial and technical inventions. In fact, though *Astérix* debuted with the first issue, the early covers of *Pilote* are photographs, often depicting moments of technological wonders.

Pilote was an ambitious and costly experiment for Dargaud, its publisher (after 1960). It went through several failing formulas in its early years, including an ill-fated attempt in 1963 to capitalize on the craze for "yé-yé" music—a sarcastic rendition of "yeah, yeah," designating pop music influenced by British and American performers (Michallat 2018). Goscinny and Charlier were installed as editors in chief that year to rescue their failing creation, and they did so by making comics the main attraction of the publication. Soon afterward, *Astérix* became a massive cultural phenomenon, arguably the first French comic to receive such attention, and *Pilote* became one of the most successful and influential comics magazines of the era.

Blueberry

Blueberry was introduced in *Pilote*, issue 210, on October 31, 1963, under the name *Fort Navajo*—suggesting an ensemble cast that was quickly discarded—drawn by Giraud under a transparent pen name, *Gir*. The series appeared on the painted cover of the issue as a "new drawn adventure." In the issue, the first two-page episode coexisted with humor series, often including adventure elements, and with other "realistic" adventure serials in established genres: pirates (Barbe Rouge), exotic adventures (Jacques le Gall), and air pilot stories (Michel Tanguy). All of these, like Blueberry itself, were written by Jean-Michel Charlier (1924–89), the other *Pilote* cofounder and a tireless provider of popular narratives since the 1950s. Blueberry mashed together Jerry Spring and the military setting of Michel Tanguy, in which Charlier had already been exploring the tension between a military structure and the impulse toward independence of typical adventure heroes. Visually, it also followed the regular layout of the other *Pilote* serials with four strips (a few series had five) and two to four panels per strip plus some space on top of the page for the title and a short summary, within the large pages of the magazine (24 × 31 cm).

Like many other French comics heroes of the postwar era, Blueberry acculturated a Hollywood figure, the roguish Westerner, complete with an English-sounding name; starting with issue 211, the title of the series even appeared superimposed on the US flag. The series was thus a reflection of the appetite for all things American—an ad on the page following the first episode offers young readers a chance "to build Cape Canaveral in their living room"—but also of the ubiquitous intermediality in *Pilote*'s content. The magazine had been launched with a radio partnership; it published photo adaptations of US films in most issues, as well as serialized novels from the Bob Morane series, through the lens of the eponymous TV show. It was, other words, quite unremarkable for comics in *Pilote* to exist on the wide spectrum ranging from intertextual reference to straight adaptations, especially from American sources.

Charlier constructs a familiar story with these building blocks, drawing from numerous Hollywood films, notably John Ford's 1948 *Fort Apache*. Blueberry is introduced in the first page of *Fort Navajo* as an unnamed poker player, accused of cheating in a saloon. Out of his uniform "to be able to cheat freely," he horrifies the young, blond lieutenant of the US Army who tries to rescue him—Craig, fresh out of West Point—when he reveals that they have both been assigned to serve in Fort Navajo, in Arizona. Though comically mismatched, the pair predictably come to an agreement over the course of the story, with Craig revealing his genuine bravery and Blueberry discarding his cynicism for the sake of a pretty young lady. Both men come to investigate an attack by Apaches, and the first set piece of the story features an epic chase on horseback, during which Giraud introduces a few larger, spectacular panels. Upon arriving at Fort Navajo, they discover that the military leadership is divided between negotiating with the Apaches and going to war with them. Over the objections of the heroes, the army sets a trap for Cochise, which he escapes with Craig's help, ending the adventure with a "to be continued," on the eve of a new Indian war.

Charlier and Giraud tell the story mostly from the perspective of the two white heroes and makes abundant use of established types (Blueberry/Craig, an unnamed Apache warmonger/Cochise, young Miss Dickson/her disapproving aunt, etc.). However, the Apaches are portrayed in a somewhat sympathetic way, especially during an attack on unsuspecting women and children by the US Army, which would not be out of place in later revisionist Westerns.

Notwithstanding these progressive moments, early Blueberry was not exceptional. Quite the contrary, it conformed to expected patterns, at the level of the French comics market and of *Pilote* specifically, offering a well-rounded but typical adventure in a well-trodden setting. By contrast, when the series ended in its run in the magazine in 1973, after ten years, it was the last of the adventure strips published there, and Giraud was celebrated as one of the best artists working in the field (Giraud and Moliterni 1970). This stunning growth in stature reflected Giraud's own development.

Blueberry was the first recurring character Giraud had drawn since Frank et Jérémie, the humor cowboy series in *Far West*, back in 1956, and the limits of his craftsmanship are immediately apparent. Blueberry's face is modeled after Jean-Paul Belmondo, then a dashing sensation in Nouvelle Vague movies,[7] but is noticeably inconsistent from panel to panel. More broadly, the story offers a wide array of styles and tones. In the early pages, background characters are stylized into sketchy cartoonish figures resembling Giraud's early humor work, while the main characters are stiffly delineated with thick black outlines reminiscent of Jijé's style and of the aforementioned *Cœurs Vaillant* cover. Some of the background elements, such as cactuses and grass, similarly come straight from Jijé's rendition (Labarre 2022b). By contrast, most of the horses are already distinct from those drawn by his master.

As suggested by Daniel Pizzoli in his meticulous study of Giraud's style, they are captured "in a few brushstrokes whose surprising simplicity and accuracy resemble the vigorous syntheses of Japanese drawings" (1995, 12). In this, they resemble Giraud's horses in *Cœurs Vaillants*, seven years earlier, though the sketchiness of individual lines cohere more effectively than in previous work. *Fort Navajo* thus offers a snapshot of Giraud's artistic evolution, filtering his own style through Jijé's teachings but not eschewing it entirely.

This is, in other words, a competent story, a fine example of journeyman's work, immediately after the end of an apprenticeship. *Pilote* seemed to think so as well, for while most of the pages were published in full color, a few episodes appeared in a cheaper format, in two colors, with red and gray wash over black ink. While roughly half the magazine was printed this way, serialized stories were typically printed with one technology from beginning to end. The album edition, published in 1965 with a cover by Jijé, was also colored inconsistently and does a poor job of covering up the discrepancies in the original publication (see pp. 25–26 for an example of pages originally printed in bichromy).[8] Conversely, Dargaud did not collect all the *Pilote* series into albums at that time: the series was likely appreciated but not a priority.

Four weeks after completing the publication of *Fort Navajo*, *Pilote* started serializing a second episode of the series, *Thunder in the West* (*Tonnerre à l'Ouest*, 1964).[9] And after that story ended, the next episode started after a three-week break. Then again. And again. The breaks became longer after 1968, but the first ten albums were produced in five years, with little to no interruptions. By August 1973, Charlier and Giraud had published the equivalent of sixteen full-color albums, about nine hundred pages, in less than ten years. Charlier wrote the Blueberry stories with the album format in mind—forty-six pages for a narrative arc, a standard length—but they also functioned as a nearly continuing serial, present in four out of five issues. Furthermore, while in traditional US comic book production, the main artist only produces a penciled version, which collaborators then ink, letter, and color, Giraud, like most French comics artists, inked and lettered the pages himself, while being involved in the coloring. Producing two large pages of Blueberry a week over several years, with increasingly ambitious penciling and inking, resembled the demanding schedule imposed on creators of the spectacular prewar US newspaper comic strips.

Faced with this rhythm, Giraud could have relied on acquired mannerisms. Instead, the early albums demonstrate a willingness to experiment and to constantly tweak his graphic choices. During the second half of *Thunder in the West*, Giraud traveled briefly to the United States, and was replaced by Jijé for a few weeks. These pages, drawn in a somewhat hurried version of Jijé's usual style demonstrate the extent to which Giraud was moving away from his inspiration: by contrast with the rest of the story, the stiffness and stylization of Jijé's characters, in particular, come to resemble the sharp profiles of Chester Gould's faces in *Dick Tracy*. When Jijé again took over from Giraud the next year, for half of *The Lost Rider* (*Le Cavalier Perdu*, 1965), he had to change his style considerably, for fear of creating too strong a discrepancy. In a characteristically genial way, Jijé later said he had learned much from the experience (Ratier 2012), but the difference between these two replacements is a good indication of the speed at which Giraud was transforming his own style. In the following story, *The Trail of the Navajos* (*La Piste des Navajos*, 1965–66), he also took over the coloring of the series, which in turn gave him an increased control over its visual aspects. For instance, instead of using deep brush strokes to suggest darkness, he renders a night scene in blue hues, drawing on the conventions of day-for-night in filmmaking, an effect that he could not have achieved up to that point.

Giraud's artistic growth through the *Pilote* era is noticeable everywhere, from the consistency of the inking within each story, to the increased dynamism of framing within panels, to the greater range of layouts in use, to the expressiveness of the character. It is, however, nowhere as obvious as in his depiction of natural environments. The early stories are unremarkable in that regard, positioning the natural world as a background, done in contour line with rough shadows and minimal texture. By the late 1960s, as observed by Christophe Blain in his comments on his own version of Blueberry, "Giraud was the greatest drawer of rocks ever" ("Christophe Blain, dessiner le temps" exhibit, Angoulême, March 2022). The rocky landscapes became prominent in his work around *The Trail of the Navajos*, two years into the series, and culminated in the two albums published in 1969 and 1970, *The Lost Dutchman's Mine* (*La Mine de l'Allemand Perdu*) and *The Ghost with the Golden Bullets* (*Le Spectre aux balles d'or*), with an extended climax in a deserted mesa. In these two stories—frequently described by critics and by Giraud himself as the apex of the series—the landscape is arguably the main protagonist, dwarfing the series' ostensible heroes and drawing Charlier's plot toward the metaphysical. Inking with a combination of brush and pen, Giraud modeled every surface, from the mountains to the characters' hands and faces with deep blacks and innumerous shorter lines, reaching an unprecedented density (Pizzoli 1995, 19–20) within organic and supple contours.

However, the final pages of *The Ghost with the Golden Bullets* differ from the style used throughout the story, featuring looser inking and figure work. Later albums in the *Pilote* era, in particular the final volume, *The Outlaw* (*Le Hors-la-loi*, serialized in 1973) move even further away from textured perfection, in favor of thicker brush lines and somewhat sketchier environments. Even before *The Lost Dutchman's Mine*, the series did not evolve in a fixed direction, but took sharp visual turns. Some of these reflect Giraud's choices, while others may have more to do with the condition of productions. For instance, *The Trail of the Sioux* (*La Piste des Sioux*, 1967–68) is noticeably sketchier than the preceding and following stories. Not coincidentally, it was also produced at a time when Giraud had started even more Blueberry: a series of small-format black-and-white adventure for the *Pilote Pocket* digests (later collected as Young Blueberry). Likewise, *The Outlaw* marked the end of Giraud's involvement with *Pilote*, and was serialized at a time when he had begun pursuing other interests. It may be tempting to think of these two examples as compromised works, sacrificing the artist's potential for the sake of pragmatic consideration. While not entirely untrue, such a view disregards the fact that published comics are always created within specific material and institutional constraints. The page format in *Pilote* is such as an example, so obvious as to become invisible, except perhaps by contrast with *Pilote Pocket*. In this much smaller format, Giraud simplified his style drastically, in what his future collaborator on *The Incal*, Yves Chaland, described as a quest for efficiency: "The brush flies at a breakneck pace on the smooth, white page. The line work is sparse and efficient. No graphic or aesthetic research: everything is boiled down to the essentials. It's clear, it's great, it's perfect" (*Métal Hurlant*, issue 39, March 1979).

In both cases, Giraud was coping with various constraints, and never producing comics for their own sakes. The meticulous numbering of the pages, or rather of each half-page, in all the albums, serve as a reminder that these stories were always meant for publication. For all his talent, Giraud at *Pilote* worked within the system of popular publication: adding his own touches to Charlier's scripts, occasionally achieving transcendent images but working firmly *within* the genre and within the logic of serial publication, in a ten-year professional journey, from apprentice to putative master.

The Iron Horse, Page Analysis

Figure 2.4 is a spectacular and fairly typical page from an album which is itself rarely seen as exceptional within the series. As such, it constitutes a convincing example of Giraud's approach to Blueberry outside the most acclaimed stories. It demonstrates not only his growing mastery of his craft but also his willingness to exceed and expand on the requirements of the series.

Fig. 2.4. Jean-Michel Charlier, Jean Giraud, *The Iron Horse*, *Pilote*, issue 381, February 2, 1967, 33.

Though published as one page, this was drawn on two half pages—numbered 33A and 33B—taped together and measuring 45 × 34.6 cm, about 50 percent larger than the published size. The page was published in *Pilote*, issue 381, on the left-hand side but appears on the right-hand side in the collected edition. Most Blueberry albums display this kind of reformatting, which means that single, rather than double pages constitute meaningful narrative units. With seven panels, spread over four strips, the page fits into the expected form for this particular story, as all but four of its forty-six pages use between seven and ten panels.

Some of Giraud's strengths are on display here. His willingness to draw everything is especially striking considering that he was producing two pages weekly. The background in panel 4 could have been omitted without compromising the legibility of the sequence, for instance, freeing time for the demanding perspectives in panels 3 and 5. The deep shadows present in all panels are not used as time-saving devices either, though this is the case in a few other pages of the story, in which they come to resemble Alex Toth or Noel Sickles. The horses, drawn in complex poses and perspectives, serve as further proof of Giraud's ability to draw this Western staple. The striking foreshortening of the mounts in panel 5 also calls attention to the way each panel contains deep, spectacular spaces (within the wagon in 33A, outside in 33B), in which the action unfolds. Though Giraud uses conventional comics symbols—or "pictorial runes" (Forceville 2022)—sparingly, with tiny speed lines in panel 1, he resorts to a variety of diegetic elements to emphasize movements within these spaces, such as the flying chain in the foreground of panel 1, the aligned seats in panel 3, or the dust and telegraph lines in panels 5 and 6. These choices ground the page in "realism" by eschewing nondiegetic elements, while proving the kind of guidance expected from such runes. This playful sense of realism is also manifest in the contrast between the level of detail afforded to the cloths and landscapes and the much more stylized face of the villain in panel 4.

Even this far from the apex of the series, Giraud demonstrated a willingness to and to conjure fictional spaces beyond the necessity of storytelling. His excesses and the coherence of the storyworld demonstrate his willingness to embrace but also to exceed his status as a journeyman.

CHAPTER THREE

Adult Comics and the Coming of Moebius

A New *Pilote*

Pilote changed after 1968, a year of massive student unrest and profound countercultural upheavals, which also affected the French comic world. Having cultivated a teenage readership and a somewhat critical worldview, *Pilote* resonated with these transformations more than most rival comics magazines. In May, young authors from the magazine summoned René Goscinny and Jean-Michel Charlier to a bar, to confront them over the editorial line of the magazine, asking for it to be more closely in touch with current events. Goscinny came alone and was deeply wounded by the reproach. He could not understand why he was conflated with authority figures and repression, at a magazine he had launched shortly after being sacked for attempting to form a creators' union, by authors he had chosen and encouraged. Giraud was there, though he later regretted the confrontation. He was then thirty, a success within the limited confines of the magazine, and happily married to his first wife, Claudine, with whom he had two children, Hélène and Julien, in 1970 and 1973. He was not, in other words, a strikingly rebellious figure, though he was about to take his career in a much less predictable course.

Following the traumatic event, *Pilote* adjusted its editorial line. It shifted away from adventure, serious and humorous, and embraced satire with a clear *Mad* influence, leaning toward environmentalism and incorporating a softspoken but resolute criticism of French society under de Gaulle, then Pompidou, with older readers in mind. Blueberry was not directly affected by these changes, though Sergio Leone and Sam Peckinpah gradually replaced John Ford as major influences on the series, but the other Charlier adventure strips, which had made up the bulk of the magazine five years earlier, started falling out of favor.

As discussed in the previous chapter, Giraud had reduced his Blueberry output by that time but still drew the equivalent of five albums between 1970 and 1973. He had also started publishing other stories for the magazine, writing for others, playing his own role in a tongue-in-cheek Western photonovel and even illustrating a few pseudonymous Goscinny stories. In a number of cases, these stories make use of a variation on the humorous style he had used as Moebius for *Hara-Kiri*, though the influence of Jack Davis and Will Elder is less prominent. After five years dedicated solely to stylized realism, *Pilote* was offering him the opportunity to embrace both of his registers again.

All the stories published in *Pilote* around that time are credited to Gir or Giraud. However, the Moebius pseudonym itself was resurrected twice in the late 1960s. First, *Charlie Mensuel*, an outgrowth of *Hara-Kiri* with a focus on American comic strips, reprinted the 1963 and 1964 stories in 1969 and 1970, without revealing the name of the author. Like *Pilote*, *Charlie Mensuel* was in the throes of Kurtzmanolatry, and the early Moebius stories fit right in. Concurrently, Giraud started using the pen name for illustrations he published in science fiction magazine, such as *Fiction* or *Galaxie* (both connected to American magazines and both featuring numerous translations), then for science-fiction novels.

From youth, Giraud had been an avid reader of science fiction, whether in literature or in comics. However, and in spite of a few notable counterexamples, the genre played a surprisingly small role in the French comics scene at the turn of the 1950s. Adventure strips would frequently include science-fictional elements—rockets were very popular post-Sputnik—but not embrace the genre fully. In spite of his impressive range in popular fiction,

Charlier appeared to have little interest for it, and the first recurring science-fiction series in *Pilote* did not start until November 1967. At that time, Giraud's friend Mézières partnered with journalism professor Pierre Christin to produce the first adventure of the influential Valérian, in a style again influenced by Jack Davis. By that time, most of Giraud's energy in comics was taken by Blueberry, and he showed no compulsion to explore the genre, except as a stylized set for some of his humor work. In fact, in one of his first professional interviews, for the prozine *Phénix*, in 1970, he cast a doubt on his ability to master the genre: "I have so much trouble drawing a chariot wheel. Imagine if I had to do a whole fleet of flying saucers!" (Giraud and Moliterni 1970).

The answer is misleading. Though he had stayed away from flying saucers, he had in fact told Charlier in 1962 that he was interested in science fiction (Giraud et al. 1993, 10) and had been drawing increasingly elaborate illustrations in the genre since 1969. Fellow *Pilote* artist Philippe Druillet had encouraged him to seek this opportunity, and Giraud committed to this work in a style markedly different from his approach on Blueberry. Compared to the lush brushwork of his Western landscapes and cragged faces, his science-fiction illustrations often aim for a form of cold elegance, relying on the use of a nib pen and abundant hatching or cross-hatching. Most of all, these illustrations, removed from any form of continuity, served as opportunities for graphic experimentation and abrupt changes (for an overview and complete index of these illustrations, see Dutrey 2012). For instance, his first illustrations for *Galaxie*, published in 1969, include two cartoonish drawings in grey wash (issue 58)—among them an extraterrestrial gleefully holding a human skin—an astronaut done in pen nib, with stark washes that resemble the work of Alberto Breccia (issue 71), and minimalist science-fiction scenes relying almost entirely on meticulous line work (issue 69). Other works on the same period, in particular his endpapers for the book collection Club du livre d'anticipation, used an extra color to further build volume or atmosphere.

As demonstrated by Daniel Pizzoli, in his extensive study of these illustrations, these various attempts display a visible debt to previous science-fiction illustrators (see fig. 3.1). In particular, Giraud borrowed design elements and rendering strategies from Virgil Finlay (1914–71), famous for his black-and-white illustrations in *Weird Tales*, whose work had been published in France in *Galaxie* (Pizzoli 2013, 12). Jijé points out that Giraud did not learn to draw from life, but rather from channeling cinema, photographs, and other artists through his own vision (Gir 1981, 7). Accordingly, his entry into "serious" science fiction, as opposed to the brief *Hara-Kiri* gags, led him to seek and integrate a new, appropriate model. Giraud never tried to hide this inspiration, and Finlay's distinctive pointillist approach—creating volume and shading through clusters of black dots—was probably recognizable to readers of *Galaxie* at the time. Though he made use of various styles in these illustrations, these black dots, combined with careful hatching, became the most recognizable feature of his science-fiction work in comics in the following years.

Underground Comix, *Actuel*, and *L'Écho des Savanes*

While 1968 shook up *Pilote* and Goscinny, a more severe aftershock followed four years later. In 1972, three of the magazine's authors—Nikita Mandryka, Marcel Gotlib, and Claire Bretécher—departed to create their own publication, *L'Écho des Savanes*. According to Pascal Ory, Giraud should have been part of that group, but Bretécher opposed the idea (2007, 240), and his work only appeared in the magazine with issue 8, two years later.

L'Écho des Savanes was a weird endeavor. Small, printed in black and white, and with an initial print run of only five thousand copies, it could barely aspire to compete with *Pilote*'s excellent production values and massive distribution. Yet, the three authors felt stifled under Goscinny's direction, and in spite of the magazine's evolution toward an adult readership, they sought to produce more

Fig. 3.1. Jean Giraud, as Moebius, illustration for Edmond Hamilton's *Starwolf*, Club du livre d'anticipation, no. 31, 1971.

personal comics. For the first few issues, the result was a mix of obscenity, in-jokes, surrealism, and psychoanalysis, with a healthy helping of the now customary Kurtzmanonaltry, all produced by the three founders.

In many ways, *L'Écho des Savanes* resembled American underground comics. It was self-published, relied on amateur distribution, and sought to imbue every line and every word contained in its pages with the authors' personalities. The founders of the magazine had access to their American counterparts: by that time, Crumb's work was well known in France, having been abundantly published in the mass-market countercultural magazine *Actuel* since 1970. Actual underground comics could also be found at newsagents in Paris, either as direct imports or in the form of Dutch reprints (Glénat-Guttin 1971, 49). With the release of Ralph Bakshi's scandalous *Fritz the Cat* movie in November 1972, seven months after its American release, underground comics and their by-products became even more visible.

However, French comics creators appear to have been inspired less by specific American comics and creators than by their aspiration to creative autonomy (Ory 2007, 240). For instance, the early issues of *L'Écho des Savanes* display a measure of irony toward the idea of the underground—creatively misspelled to reflect the English pronunciation for French readers—and contain no reference to Crumb, Shelton, or others. Mainstream French comics magazines may have been constraining and self-censored, but they were not constraining and self-censored in the same way as mainstream American comics. In the late 1960s and early 1970s, they were in fact open to a much wider variety of content and styles, while the Vietnam War and domestic violence—central issues for the US counterculture—were not as prominent in France as in the United States. As a result of these factors and a myriad of other differences, in the distribution system, for instance, taboo breaking and the claim for creative autonomy took different shapes in the two countries. And as other magazines and fanzines followed *L'Écho des Savanes*, they helped create thriving local scene, offering free advertisement and mutual reviews, sharing authors and inspirations rather than turning toward foreign publications. They did not import American underground comics so much as they transposed their philosophy in a substantially different context and on a much more limited scale (Boltanski 1975, 50; Blanchet 2006).

In common with their US counterparts, however, these comics played a significant role in foregrounding the idea of the comics author, as opposed to the comics characters or the magazines. Giraud's comics after the end of his initial run on Blueberry reflected this shift.

Bedephilia and the Comics Author

Throughout the 1960s, *Pilote* credited its authors systematically. Goscinny had fought hard in the 1950s to gain public and contractual recognition for comics writers, and his magazine reflected this, mentioning the names of artists and writers with every story (though other functions, such as the colorist or the letterer remained unacknowledged). Slightly over a year after Blueberry debuted, *Pilote* dedicated a whole issue in March 1965 (issue 283), to *La BD de A à Z* (Comics from A to Z). The issue contained actual details on the writing, drawing, and printing of comics, as well as entire sections on a mock-sociological profile of comics creators. *Pilote*, in other words, publicized its authors and made them familiar components in the experience of the magazine. However, these authors were understood as part of a larger collective. In standalone features and in series such as Greg's Achille Talon, they were often described as "a swell bunch of buddies" ("une chouette bande de copains") working together for a common goal, under the benevolent dictatorship of a diminutive but choleric Goscinny. The magazine's self-promotional discourse also emphasized topical themes—back to school, Easter, or Christmas issues—or specific stories and series, rather than specific creators.

The emphasis changed after 1968, as the magazine downplayed ongoing serialized stories and came to rely on impromptu pairings of creators for short satirical stories. Such an approach called attention to the talents involved, rather than the collective drive of the publication, and *Pilote* started including drawn portraits of the creators in the header of each page.

These changes at *Pilote* paralleled the development of critical discourses about comics, which elevated the idea of the comics *auteur*. The institutionalization of the comics fandom in France dates back to the early 1960s. Though there certainly were informal networks before that date, it is generally accepted that the creation of a *bedephile* (lovers of *bande dessinée*) movement was spurred by a 1962 article in the science-fiction magazine *Fiction*. That article, by Pierre Strinati, reminisced about the "golden age" of the 1930s, during which children's comics magazines started translating major US adventure comic strips. The text and the subsequent correspondence led to the creation of a comics society, to several fanzines and prozines (*Giff-Wiff*, 1962–67; *Alfred*, 1969–74; *Phénix*, 1966–77) and to various public events aimed at establishing the legitimacy of comics as an art form. As is often the case in such emerging fields, bedephile sought to establish the singularity of the object they were studying. Jessica Kohn has argued that bedephiles invented the idea of a comics author, while professionals in the field thought of themselves as illustrators and sought to be recognized as journalists—a much more enviable status (Kohn 2021). As is also often the case in such emerging fields, the community quickly fractured, and a splinter group led by Claude Moliterni and Pierre Couperie sought to expand bedephilia beyond its nostalgic impetus (Demange 2017).

Giraud was brought into bedephile circles by this group, as an example of modern artist who might expand bedephilia beyond its obsession with US comic strips. In 1970, for instance, blown up reproductions of Blueberry panels were shown at the Musée des arts décoratifs, in Paris, accompanied by Ennio Morricone music. These slideshows had been an important practice for bedephilia since its inception as a way to show color versions of comics masterpieces without incurring the cost of printed versions (Lesage 2022, 65). Giraud and some of his contemporaries, like Philippe Druillet, were thus positioned as heirs to "golden age" greats like Alex Raymond, whose work had been shown in similar conditions.

In 1970, Moliterni's *Phénix* put Blueberry on its cover and printed a long interview with Giraud at a time when contemporary creators still received little critical attention. This changed quickly as a second generation of bedephiles emerged, roughly at the same time as *L'Écho des Savanes*, who rejected the nostalgia of their forerunners (Mercier and Labarre 2022). Giraud found himself right in this milieu, already a fan favorite and willing to participate in various fanzines. When sociologist Luc Boltanski wrote an influential article in 1975 on the changing "field of comics" and its increasing adherence to the rules of high culture, Giraud was his prime example (Boltanski 1975). However, this newfound status was acquired in part under a different name, as Giraud brought his Moebius alias back to comics.

The Coming of Moebius

The first clear sign of cross-pollination between Giraud and his work in science fiction illustration came in late 1971, with "L'Artefact," a four-page story published in that year's *Pilote* annual. The twist-ending story is unremarkable—two astronauts discover an alien building, which turns out to be a sandcastle built by a giant extraterrestrial child—but Giraud uses Finlay's pointillist approach to shape the impressive titular artifact.

In January 1973 (issue 688), he combined these graphic explorations with a more innovative story, incorporating the challenge to classical narratives found in *L'Écho des Savanes* but also in the picaresque collages of contemporary British science fiction, such as Moorcock's Jerry Cornelius novels (whose first volume had been translated in August 1972) and in the novels of Boris Vian

(Giraud 1973, 7). The aptly named "The Detour" ("La Déviation") was published shortly before the start of *Outlaw*, his last Blueberry story for the magazine, and offered a stark departure, a detour, from the two registers he had been using in *Pilote* up to that point. Across seven pages, the story recounts a series of epic adventures befalling Giraud and his family after he decides to take a detour on the way to their vacation on the west coast of France. They encounter a "land rover," a giant whom they appease by reading a passage from Lewis Carroll, fight a fierce battle against "party poopers," have breakfast in radioactive ruins, and finally make it to their destination, represented as a flaming Mount of Doom. Giraud's self-representation falls outside of *Pilote*'s institutional framing of the magazine's "swell bunch of buddies." The Goscinny and Charlier caricatures produced by *Pilote* authors ultimately called attention to the institution itself, fictionalizing the work and the workplace in the same way Stan Lee made up a fictional Marvel bullpen in 1960s comic books. "The Detour" includes some of this, with Giraud at his drawing table, slyly advertising Blueberry and attributing a lucky escape to a vacationing *Pilote* editor. However, the story presents several realistic portraits of Giraud and his wife, Claudine, outside of *Pilote*, to the point where it provides biographical clues to careful observers (Pizzoli 2021, 18–19) (fig. 3.2). This approach fully aligns neither with *Pilote* nor with *L'Écho des Savanes*, which, like much of the US underground, invited autobiography through self-caricature, exaggerated personas, and theatrics. The centering of the artist as a statement of creative freedom is also accomplished through the story's narrative and graphic innovations.

Narratively, "The Detour" inaugurates Giraud's playful engagement with the formulas and codes of popular storytelling, of which Charlier was a master practitioner. Genres and references collide, shifting from panel to panel, while the accompanying narrative keeps a mostly straight face. However, the main draw of "The Detour" is Giraud's importation into comics of the graphic style he had been honing for his science-fiction illustrations. Working

Fig. 3.2. Jean Giraud, "The Detour," *Pilote*, issue 688, January 11, 1973.

with a nib and calibrated pens rather than a brush, he turns every panel into a graphic statement of intent. Compared to some of his illustrations, and especially to his Moebius work of the following years, he does not rely much on Finlay's dots, but the story offers "a deep dive into hatching" (Pizzoli 2021, 21). Within a bold layout, changing on every page, Giraud offers a dazzling display of his graphic palette, letting "the art proliferate to a point where it impresses the reader" (quoted in Pizzoli 2021, 21). In the space of four panels on the fourth page, for instance, he presents four portraits of Claudine and himself, which all use a different strategy to suggest the volume of the faces (sparse line, hatching, cross-hatching, and cluster of dots). The dense network of black lines, which resemble Gustave Doré's engravings much more than contemporary *Pilote* art, also succeeds in bridging the gap between photo-referenced figures (the giant) and purely imagined figures (the first panel on the fifth page, for instance).

"The Detour" was published by Giraud as Gir, but he later suggested it should have been published as Moebius (Sadoul and Giraud 2021, 176), and subsequent collections frequently bundle it with Moebius's works.[1] Presumably, so should the short and humorous science-fiction stories that he wrote and drew for *Pilote* in the following year in *Pilote* itself or in its annual. Instead, like "L'Artefact," they were published under the name of *Gyr*. Giraud still used *Gir* for Blueberry and also in his contemporary scripts for Dominique Hé, including a cannibal revision of *Robinson Crusoe*. Soon, however, the Moebius identity became the most significant alternative to Gir. While the name had heretofore served to isolate Giraud's side projects, it became his recurring alias in the French underground comics milieu. He used the identity for his first stories in *L'Écho des Savanes*, for instance, or to sign his cover for the sarcastic fanzine *Le Petit-miquet qui n'a pas peur des gros* (issue 7, 1974).

It is tempting to describe his work in these publications as science fiction, in light of his literary tastes and of what soon followed, but the label does not accurately account for the range of his production. Instead, some combination of the erotic, absurd, and fantastic characterizes most of that work, though even that broad description fails to account for the Western short he wrote for *Charlie Mensuel* (issue 67, 1974), for instance. One of his most celebrated stories in that period, "White Nightmare," published in *L'Écho des Savanes*, issue 8 (July 1974), is in fact a dry and violent account of a racist aggression in the French suburbs, in "strict observance of everyday banality" (Lecigne and Tamine 2014, 211) (fig. 3.3). The twelve-page story recounts two successive expeditions in the suburbs by a group of white racists who try to run over then beat up an Arabic-looking man. The first assault goes awry when the local residents intervene. However, this turns out to have been a nightmare, and the aggression plays out a second time: this time the man is left for dead, with residents looking on without intervening, echoing the popular (and incorrect) accounts of Kitty Genovese's murder. Fitting with the underground ethos and the prevalent aesthetics at *L'Écho des Savanes*, the story uses irregular, hand-drawn panel borders and draws attention to the gestures shaping every weird face or imperfect perspective on the page. The craft is everything but invisible, shaping an idiosyncratic and "organically expressive" (Thompson 1982, 44) storyworld in the service of political commentary.

At the graphic level, what these stories have in common is a willingness to experiment and to break away from the craggy perfection of Giraud's brushwork on Blueberry, either by foregrounding the labor of every mark (as in "The Detour") or by resorting to a sketchier, more playful approach (as in "White Nighmare"). Narratively, they also exhibit some of the traits found in "The Detour," with a playful embrace of the conventions of popular storytelling. For instance, the *Pilote* stories offer benign twists on popular genres—space explorers end up in a sand castle, a spaceship computer is obsessed with pirate tales, and so on. In "White Nightmare," the clichéd device of having the main character wake up from a bad dream is twisted into fundamental ambiguity, prompting the reader to wonder *whose* nightmare they are reading

Fig. 3.3. Jean Giraud, as Moebius, "White Nightmare," *L'Écho des Savanes*, issue 8, July 1974.

about (Lecigne and Tamine 2014). These two deviations from mainstream comics making, along with the broader underground ethos of the era, came together in his first long-form work as Moebius, *The Horny Goof* (*Le Bandard fou*).

At its core, this is typically an underground endeavor. The French title is a pun, as a "bandard" reads as slang for a perpetually horny man, but also a misspelled version of the name of a native tribe in the French translation of Lee Falk and Ray Moore's classic comic strip, *The Phantom*. The pun thus makes fun of the fascination these strips exerted on bedephiles, while relying on the expert knowledge they had helped organize. *The Horny Goof* also participates in the form of collective writing and shared jokes to be found in the budding French underground comics scene. As a form of collective writing under constraints, several authors associated with *L'Écho des Savanes* were to offer their own version of the idea (Mandryka did so in issue 4 and Francis Masse in issue 10) (Marmonnier and Poussin 2005, 24). However, Giraud exceeded these jokey expectations, by creating a long story—twenty-four pages—done in a graphic register nearly as flamboyant as that of "The Detour." *The Horny Goof* became "the tangible product of [the statement of intention of "The Detour"], the first real, full-length, adult Moebius story" (Moebius 1990).

The Horny Goof

The Horny Goof did not appear in *L'Écho des Savanes*. Instead, the magazine's fledgling publishing arm, Les Editions du Fromage, released it directly as a black-and-white softcover album in 1974. To flesh out the book, the story unfolds on right-hand pages, while on the left, a full-page flipbook depicts a man melting into an egg, which eventually hatches. The discontinuities introduced by the alternating approaches highlight the disjointed nature of the main story. As early as the title page, a big-nosed character wearing on his head a cross between a fez and Peruvian hat finds himself afflicted with an enormous erection. After failing to put it down, using threats, a stick, and some water, he runs away to avoid prosecution for this off-season erection. The plot thickens when Lady Kowalsky, a large-chested aristocrat, has the horny goof transported to her spaceship in a Dumbo-shaped shuttle, triggering an intergalactic war and over 2 billion casualties in the process. After a brief time-travel escapade, the horny goof triumphantly displays his erect penis to Kowalsky's friends on her private asteroid.

This is, in other words, a silly story, driven by improvisation, which is more often humoristic than prurient. Lady Kowalsky's breasts, like the horny goof's penis, are so exaggeratedly large that they seem to mock the underground's sexual obsessions. Furthermore, the clashing drawing registers—some characters have realistic proportions, but the goof himself is a big-nose, loose-jointed caricature—like the clashing narrative approaches on each two-page spread, make it nearly impossible to understand *The Horny Goof* as taking place in a coherent fictional universe. Instead, it functions as a collage of puns, absurd science-fictional jargon, and self-referential jokes, held together by a bare-bones narrative and by constant graphic inventiveness. For instance, while the flipbook on left-hand pages barely works in the album format, which cannot be flipped at the appropriate speed, fans have produced animated gifs out of the scanned pages, which reveal that the twenty-four pages do function as a short, surreal animation.

Page 12 from the main story (actually the twenty-third page in the album) takes places as the horny goof and a pilot sent by Lady Kowalsky finally escape their pursuers and reach Kowalsky's spaceship (fig. 3.4).

None of the previous eleven pages uses the same layout twice, and the highly unusual vertical first panel could be hard to read, but Moebius made sure to include key information in the top quarter, aligned with the panel on the right and allowing an almost conventional reading order. The graphic continuity of the textured clouds between the two panels further emphasizes this order. The

Fig. 3.4. Jean Giraud, as Moebius, *The Horny Goof*, 1974, 23.

page thus remains legible, as the "irresponsibility" (Moebius 1990) of the plot does not encroach on the efficiency of the craft. Panel 3 repeats the same strategy, which then turns into a recursive visual joke, leading to increasingly small panels, until a final black dot (on that layout, see also Chavanne 2010, 185–86). Moebius thus offers a tongue-in-cheek demonstration of his own virtuosity by creating a delicate embedded panel structure then abusing it, to the point where it cannot remain invisible. Many other pages in *The Horny Goof* employ elaborate structures—with decorative insets, for instance (18)—but they rarely call attention so openly to their formal qualities. Thierry Groensteen argues that such an "ostentatious performance" (2007, 61) draws the reader away from the story and prompts them to process the page at the pictorial level. However, because the joke is revealed gradually and further hidden by the flattening effect of black-and white printing, this page offers a sleight-of-hand, a shift from the linear to the tabular (Hatfield 2005, 48–51), which forces the reader to adjust their expectations and calls attention to the conjurer's hand.

The page also offers examples of Moebius's intertextual and generic playfulness. The Dumbo shuttle turns the science-fictional chase scene into children's theme-park ride, even as the overall narrative revolves around an oversized erection. Panel 2 reuses the Asterix gag of the pirates whose boat is inevitably sunk by the heroes. However, the Asterix gag itself was a nod to Barbe Rouge, a realistic pirate series written by Charlier, which had appeared as early as *Pilote*, issue 1. Reusing this specific gag thus places *The Horny Goof* as an expansion of the self-referentiality at work in Goscinny and Charlier's *Pilote*. In the next panel, the goof offers further metafictional musing by observing that the story is veering back toward science fiction. Taken together, these elements position *The Horny Goof* as an extension of popular culture and mainstream storytelling, observed with fondness (as opposed to what the Air Pirates had done three years earlier in the United States [Levin 2003]) but also with a distance. In panel 2, the captain's comment about the gag being "corny" is written in English even in the French edition, as an acknowledgment of the cosmopolitan underground sensibility that informed that distance.[2]

Finally, the page works as a graphic demonstration of Moebius's craft and versatility. As we've established, the bottom of the first panel is nearly useless in the linear reading of the page. However, Moebius overloads it with details and minute renderings, from the sparse wave in the foreground to the gracile lines of the erupting water, to the dotted volume on the plume of smoke. Using a rapidograph, Moebius thus exceeds expectations and narrative necessity, making drawing itself the subject of this panel. This meticulous rendering extends to the cloud in panel 2 and to the shuttle in panel 3, before a casual fourth panel. Moebius later described *The Horny Goof* as the first part of a creative "ejaculation" in the mid-1970s (Baumann 2007). The unlikely and somewhat tongue-in-cheek metaphor should be taken seriously to refer to the spontaneous, uncontrolled, and erotic qualities of these works in which the hand and the body of the creator are visible everywhere. Indeed, throughout *The Horny Goof*, seemingly capricious examples of extreme labor follow unremarkable panels that would not have been out of place in the cramped margins of *L'Écho des Savanes* or *Mad*.

After *Pilote*

The "ejaculation" soon continued with two other works, *Arzach* and *The Airtight Garage*. Both were published in a magazine Giraud helped create in late 1974, *Métal Hurlant*, which arguably succeeded *Pilote* as the most influential comics magazine in France. Before that, however, Giraud discontinued his relationship with the periodical that had brought him his stature.

Pilote had changed deeply between 1968 and 1974. Charlier relinquished his editorial position in 1972, dissatisfied with Goscinny's attempt to turn the magazine into a French equivalent of *Mad* (Ratier 1988), though by 1974, the magazine had arguably evolved beyond *Mad*'s notorious reluctance toward political stance (Labarre 2014), with numerous covers attacking or mocking French politicians. In June 1974, the magazine shifted from a weekly to a monthly schedule, and Goscinny left in August, disillusioned with the magazine, its publisher, and its numerous departing authors (Ory 2007, 240–43). Giraud's final work for *Pilote* in that period came in July 1974, an illustrated review of recent science fiction books in the second monthly issue, and his last Blueberry pages, for *The Outlaw*, had appeared in the magazine almost a year before. *The Horny Goof*—written and drawn the same time as *The Outlaw* (Moebius 1990)—was published by Les Editions du Fromage in the second half of 1974, and Giraud also published most of his contributions to *L'Écho des Savanes* and to comics fanzines in the following months.

The break with *Pilote* had been simmering for a long time. Giraud had even gone into a shooting match with Goscinny over the presence of overly traditional series in the magazine (Ory 2007, 241; Moebius 1999, 158–59). His eventual departure marked the end of a transitional period, which started in 1971 with his first science-fiction stories for *Pilote*. His Moebius identity had primarily been associated with illustrations up to that point, but in a few months, the signature appeared on such substantial comics work as "White Nightmare" and *The Horny Goof*. The transition happening that summer is neatly encapsulated by the serial he published in the popular daily *France-Soir*, from July 16 to July 20. *France-Soir*, which sold about six hundred thousand copies (Tellier 2021), had invited a stellar selection of comics authors (Fred, Alexis, Ribera, Forest, Tardi, and Giraud) to illustrate the theme of holidays. Giraud produced an absurd short tale about the hunting of a vacationing Frenchman on a pier, and though the first five pages are signed as Giraud, the final one is attributed to Moebius.

Nevertheless, Giraud did not abandon Gir, or Blueberry. Although the final story of that period, *Angel Face*, was published by one of *Pilote*'s historical rivals, *Le Journal de Tintin* (then under the title *Le Nouveau Tintin*),[3] in the second half of 1975, it continued the story and resolved a cliffhanger from *The Outlaw*. The delayed publication in album form further smoothed away the change, as Dargaud published the previous two Blueberry stories in 1974, then *Angel Face* as the conclusion of a five-album story arc, in 1975.

The choice to continue a traditional series, in a very traditional magazine, after having bemoaned *Pilote*'s "suffocating" conservatism (Thompson and Giraud 1987, 94) was in part a financial compromise. Blueberry's success allowed Giraud to pursue less profitable work (Sadoul and Giraud 1974, 9; Thompson and Giraud 1987, 91; Ratier et al. 1993, 7). Additionally, *Angel Face* demonstrated the way elements of his newfound freedom as Moebius could be folded back into his work as Gir. While *The Outlaw* was loosely drawn, almost sketchy in places, *Angel Face* offers the most fully realized urban environment of the series up to that point, often done in meticulous nib work, similar to his visual bravado as Moebius. The story also includes slapstick comedy (28), bold use of caricature, a silent fight scene, which must have cost the notoriously wordy Charlier a lot (44–45), and even a previously unthinkable hint of eroticism (23–24). The influence of Sam Peckinpah's grotesque New Hollywood Westerns is also on full display, bringing an intericonic, revisionist flair to the story, which ends with Blueberry missing in action. In a 1974 interview, Giraud reaffirmed his pleasure in drawing the series and emphasized his increasing role in the writing (Sadoul and Giraud 1974, 9), later confirming that some of the most distinctive passages in that album, in particular the most erotically charged, were improvised while Charlier was unavailable (Sadoul and Giraud 2021, 158–59). As illustrated by the unstable use of his various pseudonyms (*Gir*, *Gyr*, *Moebius*), he also had not yet fully articulated his various creative personas. *Angel Face* resembles the Moebius stories more than any Blueberry albums before or until Charlier's death in 1989.

However, in the next four years, Giraud did not produce a new Blueberry album and nearly stopped using his Gir alias. Moebius became his main identity and made him an international comics star.

Becoming an International Artist

Founding *Métal Hurlant*

In the words of Jean-Pierre Dionnet, Giraud saw the creation of *Métal Hurlant* as a way for Moebius to "become real" (Marmonnier and Poussin 2005, 34). Instead of producing a smattering of work for various outlets, some of which with minuscule distribution, he would be able to focus his effort on one magazine, whose direction he would help control.

Métal Hurlant (Screaming Metal), was devised as quarterly spin-off of *L'Écho des Savanes*, advertised in issue 9 (4th trimester, 1974) as "The first science fiction comics magazines. Coming soon to your inner screens." The claim is inaccurate since small format publications dedicated to the genre had been running since the 1950s, and Mandryka even wanted the magazine's appearance to resemble one of these cheap comics (Marmonnier and Poussin 2005, 25). However, the ad calls attention to the fact that science fiction was exploding again, after a moment of eclipse in the 1960s (Christin, Bilal, and Pomerleau 1989, 64). Comics authors of Giraud's generation were keen readers of Lovecraft and of British writers such as Ballard and Moorcock, who had shaken up the genre at both the aesthetic and institutional levels, by breaking radically with the pulp tradition. In France, the literary status of science fiction was changing as well, with the creation of hardback, elegant collections such as the Club du livre d'anticipation (1965), for which Moebius had done covers and inside illustrations. *Pilote*, for its part, started putting out special science fiction issues, both before and after the shift to monthly publication in 1974. Comics and science fiction were thus on a conjoined path toward legitimization and mainstream acceptance; the two fields intersected on many levels. Reflecting on this period in the early 1990s, Giraud stated: "At the time, our work was organized around three pillars. The first was the desire to make experimental and creative science fiction. The second was the US underground, which we were all steeped in. And the third was the French literary tradition of launching a magazine in which you can find between the lines your own way of thinking and talking, in a language that's going to be insolent, new and provocative" (Giraud et al. 1993, 32).

Born of *L'Écho des Savanes*, *Métal Hurlant* was going to be that magazine. However, *L'Echo* found itself in dire financial and creative straits before its spin-offs could be launched. Its distributor went bankrupt, and dissension arose among the founders. By the end of 1974, only Mandryka remained, at the head of a much-changed magazine. Meanwhile, the people who had been involved in developing *Métal Hurlant*—Philippe Druillet, Giraud, and comics writer, journalist and jack-of-all-trades Jean-Pierre Dionnet—began to shop the project around among publishers with ties to the underground, as opposed to established comics publishers. They went first to *Actuel* magazine, known for translating Crumb, then to music magazine *Rock & Folk*, but failed to reach an agreement with either.

Eventually, and with the help of a fourth cofounder, Bernard Farkas, the only nonartist in the group, they decided to create their own publishing structure, Les Humanoïdes Associés, which would publish both the magazines and new albums. While the four partners provided the initial capital, Giraud's Blueberry money initially financed the day-to-day operation (Marmonnier and Poussin 2005, 33). Their first book, a reprint of *The Horny Goof*, published with Mandryka's generous agreement, came out in late 1974, and *Métal Hurlant*, issue 1, in January 1975.

Métal Hurlant was very different from *L'Écho des Savanes*. *L'Echo* was printed in black and white, roughly comic-book sized, and ostensibly handmade, while *Métal Hurlant*'s glossy cover, color printing (sixteen pages out of sixty-four in issue 1) and magazine size closely resembled the monthly version of *Pilote* or any other mainstream magazine. It also had a high print run of fifty-thousand copies, a fraction of the most popular children's comics magazines at the time, but several times that of *L'Echo*.[1]

Moebius was the star attraction in the first issue of *Métal Hurlant*. He painted the cover, a monster inspired by an early-twentieth century Maxfield Parrish painting—a fitting inspiration, as Parrish straddled the divide between art and commerce, between the popular and the legitimate—and occupied half of the color pages for the first episode of *Arzach*. He also contributed three black-and-white stories to the issue: a two-page story about an astronaut trying to fix a malfunctioning sex robot, only to be chased through his ship to the call of "chauvinist pig," a science-fictional collaboration scripted by Philippe Druillet, and a one-pager on the mysteries of eroticism, working in tandem with a page published in *L'Écho des Savanes*, issue 13. Together with a short text piece, eighteen of the issue's sixty-four pages (including ads and editorial matter) were his, and all three stories were signed *Moebius*. *Gir* did not appear in the magazine until 1979.

The magazine thus made Moebius "real" in part by locating the identity firmly within the genres of fantasy and science fiction. Though those had been the dominant registers in Giraud's previous works as Moebius, he had also dabbled in many other possibilities. In addition to "White Nightmare," his 1974 pages in *France-Soir* were nonsensical but set in a mundane context, for instance (though they included "the major," who was to become a central character in Moebius's science-fiction stories).

The first few issues of *Métal Hurlant* were a work in progress on every level—replaying *L'Echo*'s woes, the magazine's distributor even disappeared after issue 2, for instance—but contained major works nevertheless, with Moebius and Richard Corben's *Den* repeatedly occupying the color pages. The magazine started as a quarterly, shifted to a bimonthly with the March 1976 issue (issue 6), and then became monthly in October of the same year (issue 10). At that point, after less than two years, Giraud had published the entirety of *Arzach*, "The Long Tomorrow," reprinted "Is Man Good?" from *Pilote*, and started serializing *The Airtight Garage* (which concluded in 1979). In an editorial for issue 4, he also articulated his creative philosophy and his refusal to follow formulaic narrative structure: "I'm about to explain why I do comics without a script. . . . [. . .] There is no reason why a story has to be like a house with a door through which to enter, windows through which to look out at the trees, and a chimney for the smoke—it is easy to imagine a story in the shape of an elephant, a cornfield or the flame of a match" (Moebius 1975, trans. Ann Miller).

Giraud was uneasy about writing editorial material for the magazine, afraid that he did not sound cultivated enough (quoted in Ecken 2022, 21), but this piece remains one of the best-known examples of writing in the history of *Métal Hurlant*. The editorial, which also includes an examination of the motivations of classical stories, is itself proof of the way writing conventions could be subverted yet retain their effectiveness. In the context of Giraud's career, and so soon after the break from *Pilote*, the text reads as an example of the "insolent, new, and provocative" language to be expected from the new magazine.

Arzach and *The Airtight Garage*

Giraud's editorial should also be taken seriously as a clue to read both *Arzach* and *The Airtight Garage*, the last two segments of the "ejaculation" started with *The Horny Goof*. Perhaps encouraged by his multiple participation in *Tac au Tac* (1969–75), a French TV show focused on improvisational, collaborative drawing, which led him to work alongside Jijé, Neal Adams, Joe Kubert, Bill Elder, Jack Davis, and Harvey Kurtzman, Giraud opened up to improvisation and unusual narrative structures more than he had done in the past.

Arzach, which appeared with a different spelling in each of the five issues, is composed of a series of loosely connected silent tales. Most of them feature a taciturn rider on a white pterodactyl (or "pterodelph"), in a vividly rendered world of science fantasy, though the series also encompasses isolated illustrations and even a two-page gag about illicit urination and the monstrous danger thereof. Narratively, the stories include classical twist-ending tales (a beautiful woman, glanced through a window, turns out to be a monster, for instance) as well as cryptic ones (an engineer driving a car resembling a Ford T fixes a machine that seems to power the pterodactyl). Even more so than in "The Detour" or *The Horny Goof*, however, Moebius's art exceeds and transcends the story. *Arzach*'s pages are drawn in nib and brilliant direct colors, depicting a lush world whose entire surface is modeled by hatching and dots. Though borrowing a creature from Finlay and many elements from French comics science-fiction pioneer Raymond Poïvet's obscure masterpiece, "M.I.X. 315" (Lefèvre-Vakana 2011), Moebius unites these various sources in a display of virtuosity, relying on labor-intensive techniques. In figure 4.1, for instance, the back of the man in the fourth panel reuses the meticulous delineation of volume that Giraud had used for his Finlay-inspired science-fiction covers (and the same photo reference; see fig.3.1), while the first panel offers wood and rock textures that rival the most elaborate Blueberry pages. Meanwhile, the irregular panels and the superimposed figure of the rider exhibit a joyous disregard for the traditional composition of mainstream comics pages. With no dialogue and none of Moebius's self-deriding witticisms, the art becomes the focal point, a statement of autonomy that encapsulates Giraud's attempt to carve a unique status for himself within the industry: "What 'Arzach' represented was the artist seizing his own freedom [. . .] freeing the artist from an inbred system of production with an excessively standardized style imposed from above" (Thompson and Giraud 1987, 110).

Fig. 4.1. Jean Giraud, as Moebius, *Arzach*, *Métal Hurlant*, issue 1, January 1975.

The genesis of *The Airtight Garage* illustrates the benefits for Giraud of working with like-minded peers. *Arzach* may be read as attempt to outdo Philippe Druillet's fantastical worlds, drawn at an enormous scale for *Pilote* then *Métal Hurlant*, which had made him a star and which Giraud had admired at once (Giraud 1973, 7; Druillet and Léturgie 1979, 19). *The Airtight Garage*, for its part, resulted from Jean-Pierre Dionnet's willingness to push his Moebius work even further toward improvisation. In an oft-told story, Dionnet visited Giraud's studio and rummaged through his sketches, unearthing a two-page "graphic joke," a "fleeting vision" in which a repairman working for Jerry Cornelius—a multifaceted character created by British writer Michael Moorcock—tries and fails to fix a psychedelic machine. When Dionnet published the two pages, Giraud quickly drew two more, with only a vague memory of the first episode, and tacked on a "to be continued" mention. By the third episode, he brought in Major Grubert, notably seen both in the 1974 pages for *France-Soir* and for a short story in issue 6, "Major Fatal." He then incorporated elements from *The Horny Goof*, in the course of long, convoluted story merging the Western, fantasy, science fiction, and even superheroes; specific references range from sly jokes about Jijé's work ("the bakalite" refers to the "b'akelit sorcerer," an antagonist in *Le Nègre Blanc*, a children's adventure comic from 1952) to *Iron Man* comics (Moebius 2011, 5).

The Airtight Garage is less immediately stunning than *Arzach*, which it succeeded in *Métal Hurlant*. Its early pages betray their origin as quick sketches, and the quality of the craft varies from episode to episode, in part because the pages were drawn at widely different sizes (some at 1.5 times the printing size in the magazine, others at a 1:1 scale, affording less room for details). The number of strips and the use of solid blacks and mechanical tones on each page also varies from episode to episode, but the story remains consistent in its use of black and white, with a combination of nib and technical pen. Within these parameters, critics like Daniel Pizzoli and Mahendra Singh have extolled the brilliance of the inking, which once again combines hatching, crosshatching, and pointillism (Singh 2012a; Pizzoli 2013) to create memorable images in a sparsely populated but densely textured secondary world (fig. 4.2).

The crucial difference between *The Horny Goof* and *The Airtight Garage* lies not so much in Moebius's developing skills—*The Garage*

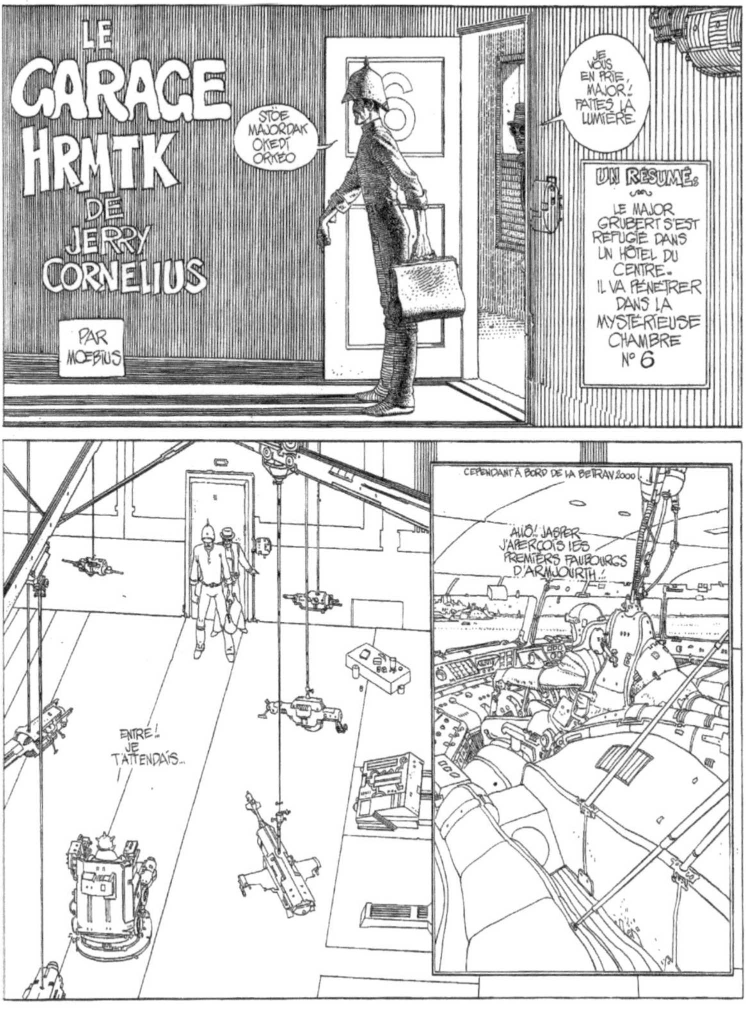

Fig. 4.2. Jean Giraud, as Moebius, *Le Garage Hermétique*, *Métal Hurlant*, issue 33, September 1978.

ended five years after the publication of its predecessor—as in their difference approach to narrative. Though largely improvised, *The Horny Goof* folded sophomoric humor into an album-long chase scene. By contrast, *The Airtight Garage* appears to build an entire world episode after episode, a three-level hollow asteroid in which every science-fictional cliché is redrawn and reexamined, to be upheld of winked at. The story mocks the conventions of serial publishing, with an ever-changing graphic design and laughingly useless plot summaries, but it does revel in plot twists and epic scenes, not all of which are undercut by distance and irony. By playing at the serial, Moebius eventually produced one.

The metaphor of the ejaculation, making the story an extension of the body, is not without merit; as Mahendra Singh notes the presence of the artist's hand on certain pages is "overwhelming" (Singh 2012b). However, Giraud more often described the process of writing the story as akin to improvisation in jazz. As Thierry Groensteen points out, improvisation is the rule rather than the exception in popular serial fiction, but Giraud's willingness to foreground free association within a flexible structure is remarkable nevertheless. The whole story revolves about major Grubert's ability to preserve the integrity of his world, and a dense layer of reference (to Moorcock, Hergé, Disney, and Lee Falk's *The Phantom*, to the contemporary fanzine scene, to central American metaphysics, etc.) makes it possible to read the entire story as a "coded diary," rife with possible psychoanalytical interpretations (Moebius 1981; Groensteen and Miller 2017). Yet, in another display of the balance between artistic independence and commercial viability, Giraud decided to offer his reader a conventional conclusion. To that end, he brought together the various narrative strands, allowing Grubert to escape in the "real" world and tying up some of the story's loose ends. In a 1996 discussion with Lewis Trondheim, soon to be a dominant figure in French comics, and who felt *The Garage* was "unique," Giraud suggested the story was a form of "compromise between madness and technique," kept within bounds so as not to lose his readers (Trondheim and Giraud 1996).

Thus, even in his "own" magazine, spurred and encouraged by like-minded creators, Giraud sought to work within the constraints of what was acceptable and publishable to his imagined readers. *Métal Hurlant* pushed the boundaries of what could be published in a mainstream comics magazine—and it was duly punished by the commission in charge of applying the 1949 law on youth publications—but it remained attached to these boundaries.

The magazine has been called a "revolution" in French comics (Pasamonik 2013), but in the history of comics as well as in the history of science (Kuhn notwithstanding), revolutions tend to vanish upon closer investigation. Moebius and the other contributors were furthering a gradual expansion of the field of comics that was taking and had been taking place in various publishing institutions. It may be more accurate to think of the magazine as a tipping point and a symbol for these changes, characteristics that subsequently enabled it to attract and aggregate emerging talents, further confirming its exceptional status. Thanks to Jean-Pierre Dionnet, and soon to rock critic and editor Philippe Manoeuvre, *Métal Hurlant* also proved eager to expand its reach beyond comics, tackling music and cinema and inscribing comics in a broader cultural scene.

Métal Hurlant might also be remembered as a revolution because, along with *(À suivre)*, it represented the final moment of centrality for French comics periodicals. Both *Arzach* and *The Airtight Garage* were designed for serial publications, and with thirty-five and ninety-seven pages, respectively, both are uneasy fits for book publication. Yet, the shift to books of comics was well underway at that time, and even at Les Humanoïdes Associés, the albums subsidized the magazine early on (Lesage 2019a; Marmonnier and Poussin 2005). On the eve of that momentous shift in the comics industry, *Métal Hurlant* shone brightly and circulated well beyond the boundaries of the French comics scene, helping turn Moebius—not Giraud—into an international star.

Heavy Metal

Giraud was not entirely unknown in the United States prior to the magazine: Gil Kane, for instance, took a keen interest in *Pilote* and Blueberry in the late 1960s (Chaykin 2016). He was also part of a collective trip by the French comics scene to the United States in 1972, during which he met the *Mad* crew as well as the younger generation of comics creators (Chaykin, Kaluta, etc.), leaving a lasting impression (Moliterni and Guégan 1972). In 1974, industry professionals awarded Blueberry the Shazam award for best foreign series, and some of his Moebius pages were exhibited in the Graham Gallery in New York in the spring of 1976. *Métal Hurlant* itself was available in a few comics stores across the country from the moment of its creation.

However, with no translation of his work available, that renown remained confidential until the launch of *Heavy Metal* in March 1977. The magazine was the result of increasing contacts between the French and US comics scenes in that decade. While French comics creators had long cultivated a fascination for the United States, the 1970s inaugurated a reciprocal movement. The boldness of French comics, their combination of high craft and underground sensibility, and the idea of selling comics as sturdy books all exerted a major influence on comics authors and publishers (Baetens and Frey 2015; Williams 2020). Twenty-First Century Communications, the publisher of *The National Lampoon*, was looking for European material, especially since translations were cheap, and Jean-Pierre Dionnet, a lifelong US comics enthusiast, dreamed of producing an American version of the magazine (Labarre 2017; 2020). These compatible ambitions resulted in a glossy magazine, which amplified *Métal Hurlant*'s innovations by removing them from their historical context (*Pilote*, *L'Écho des Savanes*, etc.) and offering them in fully developed form to US and international readers. As Benjamin Woo and Bart Beaty observe in *The Greatest Comic Book of All Time*, foreign comics can destabilize local consumption practices and lead to a revision of principles of legitimation (2016, 118). *Heavy Metal* may in fact have been closer to a revolution in US publishing than *Métal Hurlant* had been in its original environment.

Heavy Metal was not run by *Métal Hurlant* but made use of its catalog, and for about a year, the magazine relied almost exclusively on French material. Run by a minuscule team and devised as a "cash cow" (Kelly 2015), it came out the same year as *Star Wars* and *Close Encounters* and benefitted from the enormous enthusiasm for science fiction. As a result, the magazine sold roughly two hundred thousand copies a month, in a period of downturn for the comics industry. However, relations with Les Humanoïdes Associés gradually soured, with each side accusing the other of acting in bad faith, and the proportion of *Métal Hurlant* material dwindled, though it did not disappear until the demise of the French magazine, in 1987.

Initially, the magazine advertised its Frenchness as a euphemism for weirdness and eroticism. While Moebius was given as an example of that weirdness in issue 1, which also contained the first episode of *Arzach*, he was not initially given a place of choice. On the back cover of issue 3 (June 1977), his name is still written much smaller than those of American creators Robert E. Howard, Richard Corben, and Vaughn Bodé. However, as reader feedback became available, his prominence in the magazine increased. The wraparound cover for issue 4 (July 1977) is a reproduction of a page of *Arzach* (flipped horizontally), and the back cover advertises his name first, in an issue which also contains the first half of "The Long Tomorrow." From that point on, Moebius was one of the magazine's main attractions and remained thus even as relationships between 21st Century Communications and Les Humanoïdes Associés deteriorated. A collected edition of *Arzach* was among the first graphic novels published by *Heavy Metal* in the second half of 1977, reproducing the format of European softcovers one year before Will Eisner's *A Contract with God* and in a period of widespread experimentation over the idea of comics in book form (Williams 2020), followed by another volume, *Heavy Metal Presents Moebius* in 1981.

Moebius's stories quickly became admired and influential for aspiring and established artists, such as Seth, the Hernandez brothers, Walt Simonson, and Elaine and Michael Kaluta, to name but a few. In late 1977, the late underground comic *No Ducks* published a funny animal parody of *Arzarch*, "Houndzak," straight "from the milk-bone-jarring pages of Heavy Kennel," by Tim Boxell. Then, in August 1978, the second issue of Mike Friedrich's ground-level magazine *Imagine*, a sister publication to the more famous *Star*Reach*, included "Ersatz," a gentle parody of *Arzach* by Lee Marrs. The two-page story is dedicated "with best regards to Moebius" and suggests that the joke and the reference—both more indirect than in "Houndzak"—would be understood by *Imagine*'s readers, dedicated comics fans buying their magazine in specialized stores.[2] A year after the apparition of *Heavy Metal*, Moebius had thus become part of a shared comics culture in the United States. A year later, in 1979, the Japanese edition of science-fiction magazine *Starlog* started publishing translations from *Heavy Metal*, and Giraud's influence spread even further, profoundly influencing Katsuhiro Ōtomo shortly before he began to work on *Akira* (Suzuki 2022, 144).

Beyond Comics

Métal Hurlant and *Heavy Metal* also allowed Giraud's influence to spread beyond the comic world in the late 1970s, into literature and cinema. The latter would seem to be an obvious area of interest for him, given his fascination for mediated images and his reliance on the imagery of the Western in Blueberry, and he took gradual steps to bridge the gap between comics and movies. In 1970, he worked with Mézières on a hilarious Western photonovel for *Pilote*, "Les écumeurs du Montana" (issue 552), in which he plays a poor cowboy kidnapped by thugs in charge of recruiting creators for the magazine. In 1974, he was part of a mockumentary about Marcel Gotlib, directed by his *Pilote* colleague, Patrice Leconte, and according to his frequent interviewer, Numa Sadoul, was very good though the film never aired. The same year, he also drew the French poster for *S*P*Y*S* (dir. Irving Kershner) and for *Don't Touch the White Woman!* (dir. Marco Ferreri), which resemble Jack Davis's art and Blueberry respectively. When Numa Sadoul interviewed him in March 1974, Giraud claimed that he was ambivalent about making movies, afraid of the commitment such a move would require (Giraud and Sadoul 2021, 30–31). There's a striking parallel between this answer and his coyness at the idea of drawing science-fiction comics in the 1970 interview for *Phénix*. In both cases, the reluctance was soon overcome.

In the summer of 1975, in the months following the launch of *Métal Hurlant*, Giraud became involved in Alejandro Jodorowsky's planned film adaptation of *Dune*, as a designer and storyboarder. Jodorowsky was known at this point as a cult filmmaker, having directed the symbolic and surreal *El Topo* (1970) and *The Holy Mountain* (1973) in Mexico. In the 1960s, he had also published short comics, "panic fables," inspired by pop art and surrealism, some of which were published in *L'Écho des Savanes* in 1976, and, by a strange coincidence, Giraud had produced an illustration for one of his works while in Mexico, though they had never met. In 1974, a French producer, Jérome Seydoux, offered to finance Jodorowsky's ambitious film adaptation of Frank Herbert's *Dune* (1965), which had become a global success at the intersection between science fiction and the counterculture.

Much has been said about this quixotic project, notably in the 2013 documentary, *Jodorowsky's Dune*, and about the director's boundless ambitions, with a cast that would have included Salvador Dali, Orson Welles, Alain Delon, and Mick Jagger (Pavich 2013). In spite of later claims and its reputation as possibly "the greatest movie never made" (see for instance Barber 2019), nothing suggests that the film could have been made as envisioned—and haphazard organization coupled with rising preproduction costs sunk the project. However overambitious he might have been in planning for the rest of the film, Jodorowsky was both serious and astute, perhaps even visionary, in assembling the visual team for the film. British cover artist Chris Foss (1946–), whose hyperrealistic airbrushed spaceships populated the cover of science-fiction paperbacks, was brought to work with Swiss painter H. R. Giger (1940–2014) and with Jean Giraud himself. All three produced an extensive "bible" for the movie, comprising characters, vehicles, and locations, along with a complete storyboard, which now survives as a rare 268-page book and in numerous reproductions of undeniably striking images.

During the preparation of *Dune*, Giraud met with Dan O'Bannon (1946–2009), who had moved to France to supervise special effects, after having been a writer, actor, and special effects manager for John Carpenter's first feature film, *Dark Star* (1974). *Dark Star* was a blue-collar science-fiction story set in a cramped spaceship and playing underground sensibilities against the grandiose imagery of space travel, whether in real life or in movies such as *2001, A Space Odyssey* (Kubrick, 1968) or *Silent Running* (Trumbull, 1972). While waiting for the film to start shooting, O'Bannon showed Giraud a short comic he had written and drawn, featuring noir elements in a science-fictional setting. Giraud liked the story enough to offer to redraw it, and the result, "The Long Tomorrow," was published in *Métal Hurlant*, issues 6 and 7. O'Bannon did not see the final result until it was republished in *Heavy Metal* the following year (issues 4 and 5), nor did he receive any money for his involvement (Baumann 2007). The story is arguably Moebius's most influential work, though it might be more accurate to describe it as his most influential work outside the comics world. It will be examined in detail at the end of this section.

This chance encounter and Moebius's increased visibility in the United States led to more opportunities for him to work in cinema. During his idle time in Paris, O'Bannon had completed the script for what would become *Alien* (1979), reworking elements from

Dark Star and working in one of Giger's biomechanical monsters. When 20th Century Fox agreed to produce the movie in the wake of *Star Wars*, Ridley Scott reassembled the visual team from *Dune*, bringing in Giger, Foss, and Giraud, in addition to Ron Cobb, who also worked on *Dark Star* (and who was also a cartoonist, published notably in *Actuel*). In the glut of space operas that followed *Star Wars*, *Alien* stood out thanks to its emphasis on horror and to its visuals. In addition, to the creature itself, the film's science fiction world, famously described as "truckers in space," was a used-up one, a derelict and class-conscious view of the future (McIntree 2005, 29). The idea had been present in *Dark Star*, and to a certain extent in *Star Wars*, but was fully realized visually month after month in the pages of *Métal Hurlant*, in Moebius's work, and in series such as Enki Bilal and Jean-Pierre Dionnet's story of a rebel android, *Exterminator 17* (issues 11–19, 1976–77), which *Heavy Metal* soon translated. Scott repeatedly acknowledged his admiration for Moebius in contemporary interviews, but following a financial misunderstanding, Giraud worked for only two weeks on the movie, creating some of the costume designs (Fischer, O'Bannon, and Cobb 1979, 20). He later dismissed the experience as "two weeks of work, ten years of publicity and media attention" (Sadoul and Giraud 2021, 102), but Scott's professed enthusiasm in specialized magazines was certainly a factor in convincing other filmmakers to call on his talent.

Thus, in 1980, Giraud was called to work on another landmark work in visual science fiction, Steven Lisberger's *Tron*, alongside designer Syd Mead. Though Mead designed some of the film's most iconic visuals, such as the light bikes, Moebius's work is visible throughout, in the costume, the storyboard, and some of the background elements. As with *Alien*, the making-of book accompanying the movie emphasized his name, displayed his sketches, and further contributed to elevating his profile in Hollywood, leading to several instances of mercenary work in the following decade (Bonifer 1982). While the French animated feature film *Time Masters* (*Les Maîtres du temps*, René Laloux, 1982), which he storyboarded entirely, could have been given him the opportunity to shape a movie project entirely, he was surprisingly reluctant to commit to it and expressed mild disappointment about the outcome (Giraud and Sadoul 2021, 94–95). His indirect influence on the cinema was arguably more important than his direct contributions, and one *Métal Hurlant* story, in particular resonates to this day.

"The Long Tomorrow"

Katsuhiro Ōtomo, William Gibson, and Ridley Scott all specifically mention "The Long Tomorrow" as an influence on what is arguably their respective defining work, *Akira* (1982–90), *Neuromancer* (1984), and *Blade Runner* (1982) (Labarre 2022a). It thus holds a singular place in the Moebius corpus, even though he seemed to regard it as less important than his contemporary work on *Arzach* and *The Airtight Garage*.

Over sixteen pages, Moebius and O'Bannon follow Pete Club, a private detective in a futuristic vertical city, hired by an aristocratic woman to retrieve a missing suitcase. The woman is soon atrociously murdered, and Club escapes an assassination attempt of his own before discovering that the suitcase contains "the major's brain," whose disappearance could cause an intergalactic incident. The woman mysteriously reappears, and during sex, she is revealed to be a shapeshifting alien. Club shoots her and, in a melancholy final page, muses on the millions of other cases in "this city, drifting through eternity."[3] As this summary suggests, the plot follows the conventions of noir storytelling closely, with a MacGuffin, a femme fatale, a hint of class resentment, and even an equivalent to voice-over narration in the form of abundant first-person captions, such as the opening, almost parodic "I'm a private detective." The title of the story is itself an echo of Chandler's *The Long Goodbye*, published in 1953 and famously adapted by Robert Altman in 1973, understood as a metonymy for the entire hard-boiled/noir genre.

"The Long Tomorrow" fits neatly into the dominant aesthetics of Moebius's work in 1975 and 1976. It presents a meticulously detailed and textured world, drawn mostly with a nib, though a few brushstrokes are visible on page 14. As in *Arzach*, some of the modeling is achieved through vivid painted colors, though in this case, the black ink and the coloring were done on different layers and reassembled for printing. Except for a few inset panels, the story uses a conservative layout, with three or four strips per page, typically containing one or two panels. Giraud tweaks some conventions and varies the width of the gutter to emphasize a sense of time and place, for instance (p. 8 in particular), but restrains from the architectural flourish found in *The Horny Goof* or in some *Arzach* stories. The story also contains hints of his usual self-derision, with in-jokes directed toward Marcel Gotlib or funny onomatopoeias ("shock," "bump," "pomp") accompanying an otherwise serious fistfight (p. 9). However, it differs from his major works from that period in its relationship to storytelling.

"The Long Tomorrow" verges on parody, but O'Bannon's story is told with a straight face and a strong sense of its inner logic; as Giraud later described it, it worked as "a pastiche that was not a pastiche" (Moebius 1987). In this respect, it resembles Charlier's scripts for Blueberry more than the minimalist plots of *Arzach* or the improvised scripts of *The Horny Goof* or *The Airtight Garage*. Its sixteen pages also take place in one consistent multilevel setting, while Moebius's own scripts typically focus on abrupt discontinuities and magical thresholds within their unstable fictional universes. Reinforcing that logic of narrative containment, O'Bannon's script has the characters lingering and acting within specific spaces—twenty consecutive panels in Club's apartment, for instance. In other words, this is a *centripetal* story, in which narrative elements converge, as opposed to Moebius's favorite *centrifugal* narratives, defined by their constant expansion toward the margins.

The combination of these constraints with Moebius's hyper-detailed approach is a fully realized secondary world. The many spectacular panels depict a consistent fictional space, channeling Moebius's taste for graphic proliferation and noted design sense into world building that is practical more than symbolic or psychoanalytic.

The influence of the final panel on page 3 (fig. 4.3) can be felt acutely in *Blade Runner* or *Neuromancer*. It includes no less than thirty-four characters, plus a few animals, all of which have distinct clothing and occupations, conveying a sense of life in the city. Commercial signs and graffiti proliferate on the buildings (including a nod to *L'Écho des Savanes*), which recall the futuristic aspect of the Centre Georges Pompidou—then under construction in the center of Paris—under layers of grime and misuse. This is an image to get lost in, in order to take in the rust on the fire hydrant on the right, the drop leaking from the rusty pipes, or the flock of weird birds perched on the balconies. This sense of a lived-in future is accentuated by Moebius's free-hand drawing, which replaces the perfect lines of architectural blueprints with wobbly, partial, imperfect, and organic marks. This is a future of bricolage and daily life as opposed to the "modernist script" emphasizing the "lean, clean and stripped down" in typical top-down images of the future from the mid-twentieth century (Olzendiel and Zachmann 2009, 13). Giraud further emphasizes this down-to-earth perspective by positioning the reader's point of view at ground level, a common framing choice in his work, as opposed to the soaring perspectives that dominate the previous two pages.

Remarkable as it may be on its own, the panel also functions within the graphic unit of the page. As mentioned above, Giraud plays with the size of the gutter within this classic layout. Gutters are unusually thin between the first four panels, suggesting cohesiveness and—in the context of the explicit sexual tension—hinting at a form of closeness and intimacy. The larger gutter before the third strip introduces a small geographical and temporal gap, as Club travels down to the lower level from the sparsely furnished apartment. The only distinctive pieces of furniture in that place, in shades of cream and white, appear to embrace the aforementioned

Fig. 4.3. Dan O'Bannon, Jean Giraud, as Moebius, "The Long Tomorrow," *Métal Hurlant*, issue 7, 1976.

visions of the future promised by Whirlpool or General Electric in the 1950s and vividly portrayed by Wallace Wood in his adaptation of Ray Bradbury's "There Will Come Soft Rains" (written by Al Feldstein, *Weird Science*, issue 17, January–February 1953; Labarre 2018). The contrasting framing in the first two panels and especially Club's isolation in panel 2 efficiently conveys the power dynamic at the intersection of gender and class that is crucial to hard-boiled fiction, even as the text undermines the seriousness of the confrontation.

The woman's red dress and the red background (with touches of white and blue) play an obvious symbolic role, promising sex and violence, which the story delivers a few pages later. However, the color choice also serves to differentiate this luxurious apartment from the underwater green hues of the popular district on the 199th level, on the bottom strip. It also serves as a narrative guide, by priming the reader to look for red in that final panel. Club is wearing the same clothes, but has regained his colors in a less sterile environment. Cutting through the clutter, the color red guides the reader's eye from Club's trousers to a painting on the wall, to the sign for Mouna's bar, and from there toward the edge of the page. Later in the story, in a good example of the aforementioned centripetal logic at work, Giraud revives this color scheme by having Club dress in red, white, and blue, after discovering the woman's body. With sixteen such pages and the promise of millions of stories like this, "The Long Tomorrow" thus offered a novel but recognizable and above all fully realized science-fiction world, which inspired not only the aforementioned creators but also Giraud himself at the beginning of the 1980s, when he started drawing *The Incal*.

A Busy Man

As the 1970s drew to a close, Giraud was more productive than ever. He had initially hoped that getting away from the pressure of drawing Blueberry pages each week would alleviate his workload, but by the end of the decade, he was producing new books as Moebius as well as Gir. By 1979, he had contributed to every issue of *Métal Hurlant* (he missed only one between issue 1 and issue 41), and had resumed working on Blueberry. He had started *Broken Nose* immediately after *Angel Face*, in 1975, but a contractual disagreement led him to suspend the work in time for his most productive period as Moebius. *Broken Nose* was serialized in both *Super-As* and *Métal Hurlant* over three issues in early 1979, making it his first work as Gir to appear in the magazine. In the meantime, he had also cocreated another cowboy series with Jean-Michel Charlier, *Jim Cutlass*. Cutlass first appeared in 1976, in a seventeen-page story for *Pilote* (issue 25 bis). It was drawn in the quick, sketchy style that Giraud had last used for his *Pilote Super Pocket* stories nearly a decade earlier and that Dargaud had just collected as an album, rather than the more demanding art of recent Blueberry albums. The initial short was expanded, and the sixty-page album, *Mississippi River*, was published by Les Humanoïdes Associés in 1979. Additionally, Giraud began producing advertising imagery, such as a 1977 campaign for the French shoe retailer Eram, in a cartoony style and as Moebius. At the end of the decade, while achieving commercial successes across media, and under various identities, he was also embraced by critics as a key creator in the fledgling comics canon.

CHAPTER FIVE

A Celebrated Artist. A Shifting Style. A Genius?

In 1980, Les Humanoïdes Associés began publishing a hardback collection of Moebius's "complete work." Five other volumes followed until 1985, visually unified by a simple colored frame, to create a handsome and eminently collectable set. A second collection, using a similar presentation with a different color scheme, began collecting Gir's "works" (mostly juvenilia) in 1981, sold with a sticker reminding readers that this was "by the artist of Blueberry," though that attempt only lasted for two books. The sturdy volumes of these twin collections constituted a bold, unprecedented move: canonizing a living comics author, with work published mostly since 1973 in the case of Moebius. This was a striking departure from usual publishing practices as collected editions of comics up to that point tended to focus on long-running comic strips and on specific titles or characters, rather than on specific authors. Furthermore, the volumes included original introductions and a detailed origin of the various stories they contained, offering a para-scholarly approach to Giraud's work.

Of course, the collection should be understood in part as a self-promotional effort by a publisher, further elevating the status of its most celebrated author; Druillet, his only potential competitor, had broken up with *Métal Hurlant* by that time (Marmonnier and Poussin 2005, 92). Les Humanoïdes Associés also undercut the seriousness of the collection, advertising it in the magazine with a tongue-in-cheek dialogue—Franz Kafka: "Probably the most interesting book since The Castle"/Moebius: "You can say that again!" (issue 52, June 1980). However, these books do suggest that

Giraud occupied a unique position in the French comics scene at that time, seventeen years after starting his first Blueberry story, in the shadow of Jijé.

The Genius

The first sign of his growing reputation came in 1967. That year, some of his Blueberry pages but also one of his short stories from *Hara-Kiri* were republished in a thick collection entitled *Les Chefs-d'œuvre de la bande dessinée*, "comics masterpieces," alongside classic authors and brilliant contemporaries and with flattering comments. In 1969, Blueberry was also deemed worthy of a brief discussion in Gérard Blanchard's pioneering but imprecise global history of comics, *Histoire de la bande dessinée*. Blanchard even included it his general chronology as a significant event for 1965 (the year of the first album), along with the creation of Warren's *Creepy* (actually started in 1964) and Jim Holdaway's *Modesty Blaise* (actually started in 1963).

As indicated in chapter 2, Giraud had become an artist of interest for the first generation of bedephiles. For instance, in two consecutive issues of the prozine *Pogo* from 1969, Pierre Couperie and Claude Moliterni described Blueberry as "certainly the best Western since Fred Harman's *Red Ryder*" (issue 3, 57)—a common comparison in these early reviews—and Edouard François called it "some of the best Westerns ever produced, and what a style!" (issue 4, 83). In both cases, these brief mentions offer praise without elaboration. Blueberry was also distinguished consistently by these fanzines and their readers. A poll of readers by Belgian fanzine *Ran Tan Plan* (issue 19) designated Blueberry as their favorite bande dessinée of 1969, though Giraud came in third among artists, behind Franquin (*Spirou*, *Gaston Lagaffe*) and Hermann (then the author of *Comanche*, another realistic Western series). *Phénix* also awarded Blueberry their prize for the best adventure comic in 1969 and 1970, while the Belgian comic convention awarded Giraud the prize for "the best foreign realistic series" in 1971. Dargaud clearly saw value in these interactions with the fan press, and the next Blueberry album was sold with a belly band touting these awards. Meanwhile, Blueberry coverage appeared in the national press, with an enthusiastic article in the left-wing daily *Combat* in June 1970 (Talibon-Lapomme 1970), praising its art and its politics. There is little doubt, then, that the series was noticed and even admired beyond the confines of *Pilote*, though that enthusiasm did not result from Giraud's art alone.

Giraud's interview by Moliterni in *Phénix*, issue 4, in 1970, became one of the earliest examples of extended critical engagement with his work. Significantly, Moliterni prefaces the interview by stating the need to introduce Giraud to *Phénix*'s readers, covering basic biographical fact first.[1] Furthermore, although the piece reads as an endorsement of Giraud's talent, with abundant reproduction of his art, including the cover, and pointed questions about his influences and his narrative choices, Moliterni does not provide any explicit judgment.

In 1973, Giraud was interviewed by *Falatoff*, a fanzine explicitly created as a counterpoint to the perceived conservatism of the previous generation of bedephiles. While a neatly crafted portrait of Blueberry had been on the cover of *Phénix* two years before, *Falatoff* chose a sketchy self-portrait of Giraud (signed "Gir"). The tone of the exchanges is also different, using the friendly address *tu* rather than the more formal *vous*, though Giraud was actually closer in age to Claude Moliterni (1932–2009) than to his younger *Falatoff* interviewers, Sylvain Insergueix and Jean-Pierre Mercier (both b. 1954). The discussion is more casual, longer, and offers significant opportunities for Giraud to develop his view of his drawing and his peers, including what sounds like an antiphrastic dig at Hermann ("I absolutely refuse the idea that it might be plagiarism" [Giraud 1973, 5]) and a long discussion about spontaneity. Though published only months after "The Detour," the interview dwells on the story, reproduces several images, and points to the possible connection with Giraud's Moebius persona as it had existed in *Hara-Kiri*. It also investigates his connection with the underground, and though Giraud expresses his admiration for Corben and for *L'Écho des Savanes*, he does not position himself as a part of that movement.[2] The whole interview reads as friendly, reverential, and retrospectively liminal. Though he had already done some of the *Pilote* short stories, Giraud did not plan to move fully into science fiction:

> If you wanted to do scifi, you would do stories like "The Detour"?
>
> Yeah, I'd like to!!! (dreamy sigh . . .) . . . really, I'd like to . . . do stories without really premeditating the genre, without knowing how the thing would evolve. [. . .] Right now, I think the best way to learn is to do what American writers do, start with short stories, then do a novel one day. (Giraud 1973, 7)

A year later, Giraud's career and the critical discourses about his work had taken a sharp turn, as evidenced by the publication of *Gir* and by his profile in the scholarly prozine, *Schtroumpf - Les Cahiers de la bande dessinée*.

Gir was the second book in the large-sized 30 × 40 collection—the name refers to its unusual dimensions—by upstart publisher Futuropolis. It followed a first book dedicated to Calvo, a brilliant but then-forgotten funny-animal creator and preceded another volume focusing on Jacques Tardi. *Gir* did not contain any new material. It reprinted "The Detour" and various science-fiction illustrations. However, it did so in an impressive format, with excellent printing on thick paper, in a book that was consciously designed not to fit existing standards (Cestac 2007, 32–33). More importantly, the series foregrounded the authors, only mentioning their names on the cover, rather than their characters. This unusual celebration of the artist was heightened in the case of *Gir* since the illustration reused one of the self-portraits from "The Detour." The book had a small print run, likely in the few hundreds (Cestac 2008, 66–67), but it offered a model for publishing comics creators as auteurs, and it designated Giraud as one of them.

In the same period, *Schtroumpf-Les Cahiers de la bande dessinée*, issue 25, printed the first extensive study of his work. The name of the publication refers to *Les Cahiers du cinéma*, where auteur theory was crafted and popularized. Accordingly, it had settled into a formula in which every issue covered a specific francophone artist in depth. The issue was published in the second half of 1974, roughly coinciding with Giraud's departure from *Pilote* and with the publication of "Cauchemar blanc," *The Horny Goof*, and *Gir*,[3] and shortly before *Métal Hurlant*.

Giraud was not the first creator of his generation to be profiled: Mézières, Gotlib, and Bretécher had preceded him, and while this should not be read as a strict order of precedence, it indicates that he was not yet perceived as singular or especially prominent among the former *Pilote* alumni. That issue of *Les Cahiers de la bande dessinée* helped change this perception, thanks to extended analyses but also to Giraud's efforts at crafting his self-image, as early as the cover. The full-figure self-portrait is drawn in his Moebius style (though signed *Gir*)—nib, not brush, with dots and short lines providing texture—brightly colored, and represents him smiling, wearing an aviator helmet, part of a jester's costume, and a kingly cape. The overall impression is of a mocking self-aggrandizement, a strategy that Marcel Gotlib had already used in issue 13. The decisive gesture comes on page 3, with an eight-page drawn interview, based on a conversation with Numa Sadoul. The questions are accurately transcribed, and the answers are initially serious, but the interviewer is not represented visually, while Giraud or an avatar thereof is present in every panel. The dialogue is turned into an exercise in self-representation.

Graphically, these pages resemble the *Falatoff* cover: again, a nib, or perhaps a rapidograph, and a sketchy, rounded register, veering between cartoon figures and more realistic portrayals (p. 6, last panel, for instance; see fig. 5.1), within organic, irregular panels. The idea of a fluid identity shaped by the artist himself is introduced in the very first panel, a full-page drawing of Giraud as an écorché, about to put on his human mask, and it is sustained throughout.

Fig. 5.1. Jean Giraud, drawn interview with Numa Sadoul, *Cahiers de la bande dessinée*, issue 25, 3rd trimester, 1974.

Even as the interview devolves into Carrollian absurdity—at one point Giraud nonsensically states: "Cinema is wormerland valle bar! Rojure dac astroven dac!"—the self-portraits and metamorphoses remain. An unknown voice correctly observes that "[the exchange] does not correspond to the *Phénix* interview at all," even though the two discussions occurred only three years apart.

With these often-reprinted pages, Giraud invents a form that resembles the self-mocking confessional tone used by many underground cartoonists, yet he invokes the authority of the outside observer—not to mention the legitimacy of *Les Cahiers de la bande dessinée*—to turn that self-image into more than whimsical self-indulgence. This is shared autofiction as critical engagement, validated by the exterior gaze. The self-derision is real, and these are genuinely funny pages, but the interview also represents an effective attempt at self-mythologizing and a powerful rebuttal to the image of the cautious craftsman projected in *Phénix* a few years earlier.

The first article following the interview analyzes Blueberry as revisionist Western, shaped by both Giraud and Charlier, but the other analytical pieces focus on Giraud, and only him, as an author. He is credited, for instance, with introducing a left-wing worldview in the heretofore "reactionary" Blueberry (Roux 1974, 35), and the whole series is described elsewhere as *his* work, with only minor concessions to the writer's contributions (Di Manno 1974). François Rivière, for his part, describes the series as a mere "launching pad" in Giraud-Moebius's career, a "parenthesis" in his exploration of the "great imaginary" of the fantastic. Far from a mere illustrator, Giraud is "more serious" than contemporary creators working in the science-fiction genre and is conscious of the interaction between comics and literature (Rivière 1974). Antoine Roux describes Giraud more bluntly as a "genius artist" (Roux 1974, 35)—the first use of the term I have been able to find, but by no means the last.

A few months earlier, Yves Frémion had lumped him with Gotlib and Mandryka among "the best of our graphic creators" (1974a,

23) and in his review of *The Horny Goof*, noted that Giraud "was peerless in his ability to conjure an entire novel in single drawing" (Frémion 1974c, 86). The next year, *L'Écho des Savanes* called him "the best drawing artist in the world" (issue 11, 49), while another comics magazine created by *Pilote* alumni, *Mormoil*, placed him alongside André Franquin and Ronald Searle—not a comic artist—in a list of the best European drawing artists (Mulatier 1975, 55). All of these articles articulate a shift in the framing of Giraud's work. From a *virtuoso* within the field and within a genre—maybe even "the best Western artist of all time," as *France-Soir* called him (*France-Soir* 1974)—he was quickly becoming a *genius*, able to transcend such boundaries and consecrated as such. By the early 1980s, this take had become consensual on both sides of the Atlantic. Reviewing *Heavy Metal Presents Moebius* in *The Comics Journal*, Kim Thompson introduces Giraud as "one of comics' undisputed geniuses" (Thompson 1982, 44).

Writing in 1975, sociologist Luc Boltanski had examined the way younger comics creators sought to redefine the status of their profession, with Giraud as one key example. Boltanski analyzes the ways in which these creators sought to imbue the field of comics with the values of "high culture," by breaking with the practices of the previous generations. He points to the various institutional practices—journals, awards, reprints, and teaching—which helped foster supporting discourses but also highlights the reluctance among these new creators to fully embrace the social definition of "the artist" (Bart Beaty echoed this observation thirty-five years later in *Comics versus Art*, 2012). Giraud is a perfect example of this break with tradition, symbolized by his leaving *Pilote* and confirmed by the wariness both Jijé and Charlier expressed toward his work as Moebius (Giraud and Sadoul 2021, 19, 221). He also comes across as warm and self-mocking in interviews, and the portrait drawn by Tardi for the cover of the first book devoted to his work—Numa Sadoul's *Mister Moebius et Docteur Gir* (1976)—is a gentle caricature: a pensive Giraud in a crumpled bourgeois suit, holding out a nib and a brush. However, this self-derision, this prudence, was gradually giving way to a still humorous but more assertive discourse about his artistry. In *Mister Moebius et Docteur Gir*, he discusses his responsibility as "the possessor of a talent, almost a 'mission'" (Sadoul and Giraud 2021, 26). By 1978, in a *France Inter* interview, he conceded to being, if not the best drawing artist in the world, at least "one of the least bad" (Renoux 1979).

This sense of self-importance was bolstered by the number of creators who sought to pay homage to his work or simply to imitate it. Though Enki Bilal has rebutted the idea, his early works, also published in *Métal Hurlant* and *Pilote*, read like an imitation of the first Moebius stories. At *Métal Hurlant*, young creators like Yves Chaland and Serge Clerc came in as admirers and helped further spread the gospel: for instance, in a portfolio published in the science-fiction magazine *Univers*, issue 15 (1978), Clerc included a full-page homage to major Grubert and the then-ongoing *Airtight Garage*. Conversely, Philippe Druillet, whom Giraud mentioned as an inspiration and even a model in early interviews (Giraud and Moliterni 1970; Giraud 1973, 6; Giraud and Sadoul 2021, 24), was mentioned more sparingly in the second half of the decade. From Druillet's perspective, Giraud benefitted from his inspiration and support early on—Druillet had notably introduced him to science-fiction publishers—but failed to give him credit in what had become a tense professional rivalry (Druillet and Alliot 2014, 122–26; Quillien, Frissen, and Druillet 2022, 120–23).

The publication of Moebius's "complete work" by Les Humanoïdes Associés (along with the publication of an art book, *Moebius 30 × 30*, with a foreword by Fellini) marks the end of a process spanning most of the decade. The field of comics in France was pivoting toward a new conception of the author, inspired by the underground and valuing personal expression and originality above the adherence to popular, serial norms. Giraud was neither the first nor the most prominent of these creators—Marcel Gotlib was probably the most important early on—but his adoption of the Moebius persona served as a powerful metonymy for the transformations of the field. Through interviews, unusual publishing projects, and of course, highly innovative comics work, all caught in mutually reinforcing feedback, he helped craft his image as an *auteur* in the course of the decade. In early 1981, he received the Grand Prize in the Angoulême Festival, essentially a lifetime achievement at the age of forty-two (his mentor, Jijé, had received it in 1977), as a further confirmation of his exceptional status in the field.

Serial Artist

In 1980, Giraud embarked in another major serial project, *The Incal,* written by Jodorowsky. Across six volumes, it follows John Difool, a private detective embroiled in a galactic struggle between light and darkness. Difool, accompanied by a miniature version of *Arzach*'s bird—who soon learns to talk—becomes the vessel of the force of light, a sentient pyramid known as the Incal. Though a reluctant hero, whose main interests lie in sex and booze, he eventually staves off the destruction of the universe with the help of a ragtag crew.

Unlike contemporary episodes of Blueberry, the series incorporates the magazine format. It includes chapter titles, for instance, which only make sense in the context of episodic publication, and according to Giraud, it was drawn and inked from beginning to end at the rate of one page a day (Sadoul and Giraud 2021, 185). This is in many ways Giraud's farewell to adult comics magazines, a market that collapsed before the end of the decade. The final volumes of the cycle, *The Fifth Essence* parts 1 and 2, were in fact published straight as albums in 1988, a year after the disappearance of *Métal Hurlant*. Though serialized, the series was also designed from the start with ulterior publication as a traditional forty-eight-page color album in mind, the first Moebius story to fit that format. Most of his earlier work, especially short stories like "The Long Tomorrow" or "Ballad" (1977), was available or about to become available in book form, but their inclusion in variously titled collections made them hard to recommend or identify. Meanwhile, neither *The Airtight Garage* nor *The Horny Goof*, both only in black and white at that point, matched the traditional format. Familiar, easily reprinted, superficially fitting the mold of so many other adventure series, *The Incal* became Moebius's most popular work for general readers, but it drew on Giraud's experience as Gir. The covers of the album state "A John Difool adventure," in the tradition of character-centric adventure strips, and the series was also Giraud's first extended collaborative work as Moebius. More broadly, its narrative structure, though seeped in mysticism, does not resemble the automatic writing and drawing of his seminal mid-1970s work; the mock recaps of *The Airtight Garage* are replaced by straightforward summaries of previous episodes, for instance. Moreover, *The Incal* was born out of *Dune*. After the collapse of the movie, Jodorowsky became a friend and philosophical mentor for Giraud. They worked together in 1978 on an eerie illustrated story, *The Eyes of the Cat* (*Les Yeux du Chat*), published in album format as a gift for buyers of Humanoïdes Associés albums, before deciding to reinvest part of what would have been in *Dune* in a sprawling, epic story. Jodorowsky did not write a full script, but he worked on the story with Giraud in joint sessions in which he would act out the main events (Marmonnier and Poussin 2005, 87). As noted by numerous commentators, the story includes echoes of Frank Herbert's novels, in particular its intermingling of mysticism and political struggle, but also more specific plot points. For instance, the late volumes include a double-cross by the private councilor of a ruler, a "mentrek," that closely resembles a similar plotline involving a "mentat" in Herbert's first novel and reuse design elements they had imagined for the movie adaptation (Alessandrini, Giraud, and Jodorowsky 1976, 96).

The early volumes of *The Incal* also resemble previous Moebius stories, in particular, "The Long Tomorrow." Both stories involve a clichéd private detective roaming in a socially stratified futuristic vertical city. The two places differ in their fashion, in the appearance of the robot police, but they offer a similar urban nightmare, and the spectacular splash page at the beginning of *The Incal*, a vertiginous fall through the city, closely mimics the equally spectacular perspectives in the first two pages of "The Long Tomorrow." Though it abandons the device quickly, *The Incal* also opens with flashback structure driven by Difool's unreliable narration in captions, fully embracing the parodic noir mode of its predecessor.

Graphically, the first two albums, serialized consecutively from December 1980 to October 1981 (*Métal Hurlant*, issues 58–68), differ markedly from the next two (1983, 1985) and even more so from the two volumes of *The 5th Essence* (1988). Early on, the series functions as a compromise between the hyperdetailed world building to be found in Giraud's mid-1970s work and the quicker, more economical line work he had experimented with in *Jim Cutlass*. The futuristic environments bear his trademark rustiness, scratches, and peeling paint, made tangible through spidery nib work, though the frequent use of a ruler makes them less unified and organic than in "The Long Tomorrow." Crowds are frequently detailed to the last individual (see fig. 5.2, or *The Luminous Incal*, 11) in a familiar display of graphic excess, which makes the storyworld and its various locations sharply differentiated and, above all, tangible. Other pages display a thicker, bolder line, with less contrast between contour lines and textures, reminiscent of the directness to be found in "White Nightmare" (*The Black Incal*, 19 is striking in that regard). Giraud also uses that thick line for characters, simplifying and typifying features to aim for expressivity rather than elegance or realism. As with *Jim Cutlass*—and the Blueberry stories for *Pilote Super Pocket*, in which he first tried this register—these are time-saving choices, making it possible to maintain the self-imposed pace of one page a day, while maintaining a degree of graphic continuity with his previous Moebius work. The first album displays many abrupt shifts in the level of detail afforded to characters and environments, sometimes in the middle of the same chapter (pp. 26–28, compared to p. 29), suggesting that Giraud was feeling his way into that rhythm, and adjusting abruptly as deadlines loomed.

Fig. 5.2. Alejandro Jodorowsky, Jean Giraud, as Moebius, *The Black Incal*, *Métal Hurlant*, issue 58, December 1980, original art.

Starting with *What Lies Beneath*, the third album, the level of detail in the background declines, even though Giraud started working at a larger page size (from 30x38 cm to 37 x 49.5 cm, or roughly from 1.5 x the printing size, to 1.85 x). As the story moves into space and embraces the *Dune* inspiration, Giraud stops drawing *everything*. He suggests what earlier albums represented (see the building in *The Fifth Essence—Planet Difool*, 20–21, for instance) and increasingly tends to omit backgrounds entirely. Characters remain drawn with simple, expressive features, but also with bolder inking, and lush contour lines inked with a brush rather than a nib. The last two albums also make use of more baroque layouts, with full-page bleeds, overlapping or borderless panels, as if to offer a new form of spectacle. These are leaner, more efficient albums, stripping down some of the graphic exuberance—the "graphic overload" (Sadoul and Giraud 2021, 117)—which carried over from Giraud's 1970s work to the first year or so of the series. However, because these six albums exist in continuity, the settings and characters remain recognizable from episode to episode, preventing Giraud from anything but incremental changes. He would push his aspiration for a simpler, sparser style in a different series, unburdened from that inheritance, immediately after the end of *The Incal*.

Mysticism

Entertaining as the series may be, it is hard to read the six volumes of *The Incal* as anything but a tale of artistic retreat. It can be explained in part by Giraud's impatience toward continuity and long-running projects. *The Incal* started as a compromise, almost a paradox: a popular series, a cocreation over which he did not have total control, notably for the coloring, which nevertheless demanded an eight-year commitment and used the Moebius identity.

During a 1988 interview with Numa Sadoul, for a new edition of *Mister Moebius et Docteur Gir*, Giraud appears somewhat detached from the series, expressing his dissatisfaction with the colors of the last three albums, but also, uncharacteristically, with his own drawing. Against Sadoul's precise criticism, he defends *Fifth Essence*, which had just been published, without much conviction: "Difool's head could have been more precise, but I find it efficient like that. [. . .] You are right that the crowd would have been more detailed, but when you have to represent thousands of people, you have to find solutions. [. . .] No, no, there are worse things in this album, and of course better ones too" (Sadoul and Giraud 2021, 185–86).

Yet, his most open admission of failure regarding the series concerns the third album, drawn and serialized in 1983: "That comic was difficult, when it came to the script, and not well made, I realize that now. I fought for a long time because people were telling me that it wasn't much good, but I have to admit it came at a time when I was not doing all that well" (Sadoul and Giraud 2021, 127).

By that time, he was deep into a phase of mysticism, which had really started back in 1975, when he met Jodorowsky. The Chilean creator, a self-described mystic and seer with a deep appetite for self-mythologization, exerted an immediate influence on Giraud, prompting him to embrace meditation, physical exercise, and vegetarianism. As early as 1975, and for the rest of his life, Giraud considered him as a master, whose teaching revealed profound truths about the universe. In 1977, Giraud left the Paris suburbs with his family and moved to the small town of Castets, in the Pyrenees, in a bid to escape a possible destruction of the city. Around the same period, he also visibly transformed his behavior and clothing, from chain-smoking urban dweller to rural New Ager. Some elements of this self-discovery process seeped into his work, in particular in *The Airtight Garage*, where they added to a hearty cultural mixture.

Giraud had also progressively drawn closer to the Iso-Zen cult, which also included fellow *Métal Hurlant* artist Sergio Macedo. He and Claudine had first met the group in 1974 or 1975, but he grew much closer to them in 1981 and 1982, while working in Romorantin after leaving Castets. Led by Jean-Paul Appel-Guéry, the cult pushed the then-common idea of extraterrestrial wisdom, found in Ron Hubbard's Scientology as well as in Erich von Däniken's best-sellers. Over time, Giraud's accounts of his belief in the teaching changed noticeably as what appeared to be earnest and literal enthusiasm turned into a more allegorical understanding of the group's aims. In 1983, he moved to Tahiti along with the rest of Iso-Zen, where he and his family apparently retained some autonomy from the rest of the group. He officially left Tahiti and the group in late 1984.

Some of the Iso-Zen teaching resonated with the spiritual craving to be found in Jodorowsky's work, and the Manichean vision of a sentient crystal—the Incal—works in both contexts, for instance. However, Iso-Zen's specific form of enlightenment, including a gradual shedding of one's personality, could not be further from Jodorowsky's exuberant celebration of artistry and creativity, his own in particular.

In the early 1980s, part of Giraud's output and fame were put to work in the service of the cult. This is clearly apparent in several interviews he gave in those years, containing passages such as: "Regarding drawing, I also want to say that lines and gestures are manifestations of ego and power. By definition, the ego is the unconscious of energy fields which go through the universe and go through us. The modern, secular artist is the bearer of certain powers but he is not aware them" (1981 interview, quoted in Moebius 1984, 97).

The injunction to get rid of one's ego triggered an evolution of his drawing style, away from the graphic overabundance of his 1970s work, and is visible in the later volumes of *The Incal* but mitigated by the constraints of a continuing series. However, the immediate effect of his belonging to the cult was a drying up of his creative potential and a ruthless exploitation of his name. The most egregious example is to be found in *La Ferme des animaux*, a comics adaptation of Orwell's *Animal Farm*, bearing his name and Marc Bati's on the cover, published in 1985.

According to his own testimony, Giraud's involvement in the project was limited to watching the 1954 animated adaptation (dir. Batchelor and Halas) and doing quick sketches of potential panels. He then passed this rough layout to other hands within the group, including Bati, who finished penciling and inking.[4] The book also appears to have been lettered if not by Giraud, at least in a sustained imitation of his work, and it bears a trademark paratextual indication, the numbering of each half-page, as seen in Blueberry. In other words, though the result is beyond pedestrian, the book masquerades as a production by Giraud.

Other works from the era, such as "La Nuit de l'étoile" (in *Métal Hurlant*, issue 98–99, 1984) function as proselytizing pieces from the sect, and in Giraud's own words, the short story "Edena" (in *L'Expansion*, 1982, with colors by Bati) was an effort at pure propaganda: "I had six pages and the total freedom to create anything I wanted. When I started to talk about it with Jean-Paul Appel-Guéry who, at the time, was a little like my spiritual advisor, we quickly arrived at the conclusion that, instead of doing a straight science fiction or fantasy story, we were going to present them with a tract, a manifesto, something like the comics the Chinese used to do under Mao, even if it was a bit of a simplistic and naïve approach" (Moebius 1987a).

Giraud also spent years trying to develop an animated feature film, *Internal Transfer*, based on a script by Appel-Guéry himself. The project never came to fruition, though a pilot including the rider from *Arzach*, was produced in 1983, and Giraud kept mentioning it throughout the decade. The attempt to produce *Internal Transfer* convinced Giraud to move to Los Angeles in 1984 and drift away from the cult. Though he never fully disowned Iso-Zen, he appeared to have regained a form of autonomy and creativity during that period, possibly with the help of psychoanalysis, to which he had been very reluctant up to that point.

However, the experience left him deeply changed. At the superficial level, this was made manifest by the recurring presence in his personal work of crystals, supreme beings, and wisdom descending from the stars, a form of piety that had no place in his earlier work. On a stylistic level, this led him to embrace a sparser line, aiming for perfection rather than exuberance.

Giraud analyzed this transformation in the art book *Venise Céleste*, in 1984, using as points of references two pillars of francophone comics, André Franquin and Hergé. Hergé, Georges Remi (1907–83), the creator of *Tintin*, probably requires no introduction.

He had been one of the most popular artists in comics since the 1930s, and he and his studio had trained many key artists over the decades, from Edgar P. Jacobs (Blake and Mortimer) to Jacques Martin (Alix), sustaining the fortune of the *Journal de Tintin* magazine and of Casterman, which published the albums. However, it is only in the 1970s that Hergé's contribution to the form and his status as an artist were analyzed and demonstrated. For instance, shortly before his Giraud book, Numa Sadoul had published the influential *Tintin et moi*, in 1975. And in the waning years of the decade, while some in the *Métal Hurlant* crowd (Yves Chaland, Serge Clerc, etc.) were rediscovering Jijé, other contemporary European creators embraced Hergé's influence. In 1977, Dutch creator Joost Swarte coined the phrase "the clear line" ("la ligne claire") to encapsulate Hergé's sense of graphic reduction and meticulous design, and the expression was subsequently adopted by artists seeking to claim that influence. Hergé's style was defined and understood precisely at the time Giraud, as Moebius, was conducting his most daring experiments.

Like many of his contemporaries, Giraud mentioned Hergé as a model in the mid-1970s, and reworked some of his characters in his illustrations for fanzines. Thierry Smolderen, who went on to become a celebrated writer and historian of comics, published a somewhat tongue-in-cheek illustrated book in 1983, *Les Carnets volés du major*, examining the many echoes between *The Airtight Garage* and *Cigars of the Pharaoh* (1934, 1955).

André Franquin's global renown does not match Hergé's, but his popularity and influence on francophone creators is equally remarkable. Trained by Jijé, like Giraud after him, Franquin (1924–97) shaped the modern incarnation of Spirou from 1946 to 1968. In 1957, he created Gaston Lagaffe—the "unemployed hero"—a kind, philosophical loafer, forever sabotaging the buttoned-up office life at a fictional version of *Le Journal de Spirou*. Like Hergé, Franquin had his own studio, in the late 1950s, and like him, he was widely admired and imitated. Unlike Hergé, however, Franquin's art relies on the extreme visibility of the artist's hand, creating a flexible and idiosyncratic world out of dexterous brushwork, embracing caricature (all his characters have memorable noses) and the ability of the contour line to suggest motion. In 1975, Jean Mulatier, himself an expert caricaturist, described Franquin and Giraud, in that order, as the best comics artists in Europe.

In *Venise Céleste*, Giraud describes his hesitation between the two models:

> Franquin understood the importance of the gesture in creative work, and among artists like Hergé, one finds a reflection about the line as a way of being. In fact, Franquin and Hergé are the two major approaches to drawings, and they correspond to broader trends which you can find in the whole history of art. [. . .] As to me, I've been fascinated by both, and I have enjoyed balancing the two. Which is why some Moebius comics have been done in that spirit they call "the clear line," which is a good definition though it only describes the end product, and neither its origin nor its totality. (Moebius 1984, 97)

Some of the later pages in *The Airtight Garage* do resemble the "premeditated line" to be found in *Tintin*, but they exhibit a formal playfulness, in the framing, in the various flourishes (in the hatching, for instance), and especially in their mutability, which makes the comparison a distant one. *Tueur de Mondes* (1979), a short tale printed as a promotional item by Les Humanoïdes Associés, hews even closer to Hergé. However, it is really in the 1980s that Giraud-Moebius embraced this type of extremely controlled production, which he likens to "sacred art" on two occasions in the same book. Some of the images in *Venise Céleste* are signed *Jean Gir*, a new pseudonym expressing a reconciliation of his real name and his artistic persona.

The image he created in 1983 to advertise the Alice personal computer, a French version of Commodore's TRS 80, offers a fine example of his new graphic approach (fig. 5.3). A young and radiant blond girl wearing a tunic, leggings, and long socks is sitting

Fig. 5.3. Jean Giraud, as Moebius, illustration for the ads and packaging of the Alice computer, 1983.

on a pile of cushions, while the computer floats in front of here. The picture is dominated by yellow and blue (and green in the packaging, though it is less prominent in the original illustration), set against the red of the computer and of the apple the girl holds in her hand. Texturing is minimal on her clothes and also on the objects around her, with a few short lines of regular width helping to shape volumes. This is a controlled image, in which the comfortable clutter in the bottom half contrasts with the serene perfection of the computer, the gradient in the sky, and the computer itself, a demonstration of Giraud's attempt to "clean-up" his art (Smolderen 1984, 90). It is also imbued with mysticism. The untouched red apple serves as the promise of a sinless world, while the star symbol on the girl's tunic echoes similar representations of illumination in Giraud's other works under the influence of Iso-Zen.

However, such an advertising picture offers its own constraints: it is meant to be striking, pretty, and recognizable as Moebius's work. Like *The Incal*, it is not entirely free from continuity. Furthermore, the "clear-line" aesthetics at its most archetypal was designed and perfected as a form of narrative drawing.

Giraud's second continuing series as Moebius, his most obvious experiment with the clear line, started as a commercial work, not unlike the illustration for the Alice. In 1983—the same year as the third volume of *The Incal*—he agreed to design a communication project for Citroën, with few constraints providing the brand was recognizable. Though he varied somewhat in his description of the initial order, Giraud consistently stated that it was not meant to become a full album, rather a short seven- or eight-page story (Ratier et al. 1993, 22–23; Sadoul and Giraud 2021, 193), which grew into a full science-fiction album; in the 1987 edition for Marvel/Epic, Giraud suggests that the thirty-nine-page story was improvised over the course of half an hour. Les Humanoïdes Associés printed 10,000 copies, 6,000 of which were distributed to Citroën clients, along with a portfolio (250 copies) and an even rarer special edition for Citroën employees (100 copies). The complete story was also published as a detachable insert in a Christmas-themed issue of *Spirou* a year later, and several additional reprints soon followed, intended for the traditional market. The promotional effort thus turned into a conventional, and successful, publication.

The story focuses on two androgynous space mechanics, Stel and Atan, who find themselves stranded on a mysterious planet along with a host of extraterrestrials, waiting around a mysterious pyramid. Eventually, the pyramid opens to Stel, revealing a radiating crystal under starry lights. The pyramid then absorbs all the travelers and turns into a dual spaceship—shaped like Citroën's logo—before disappearing into space as one final shooting star.

The themes are familiar, combining elements of Philip Jose Farmer's *Riverworld* (1971–83) with elements from *Close Encounters of the Third Kind* (1979) and Giraud's now familiar fascination with crystals and space revelations. It is also an intimate story, a travel narrative with domestic elements and a sense of companionship that had been absent from Giraud's scripts since "The Detour." As a matter of fact, when he added a short story entitled "The Repairmen" to *Upon a Star*, for the commercial album version, Giraud had Stel meet a younger version of himself in a surprisingly open autobiographical moment (as confirmed in Moebius 1999, 11–12, 56). The character enters the psyche—the core—of a biomechanical "waymaster," a giant, Godlike creature, and fixes "an old story from the past" in the form of a broken submarine. Stel then reflects that he too had a broken submarine. Giraud's publisher at the time reads the story as an allegory for psychoanalysis (Annestay 1990), with Giraud as both the Godlike waymaster and the nimbler Stel. This is, in other words, a personal story, offering a further alter ego to Giraud-Moebius, after Blueberry and Major Grubert. Proselytizing and branding may be at the heart of the book, but it is fair to say that it exceeded both these initial aims.

Giraud's clear line is built within simple, regular layouts. Pages are divided into vast panels (six at most, frequently four or less), in which the background is often absent or reduced to gradients and vast swaths of color, to represent the quasiempty planet. Even the inside of the spaceship is represented through geometrical, neatly delineated forms, with the exception of a few busy panels. On page 17, the straightforward temporal caption in the last panel also points to the use of highly conventional comics tools.

Giraud inked the panel borders as well as the word balloons with a ruler, deflecting any potential expressive quality to these lines, though they remain obviously hand drawn (other pages feature slightly looser balloons, though they are all square). He does include, however, a slightly higher gutter between the third and fourth strips—a design tool already present in "The Long Tomorrow"—in a nearly invisible tweak on the traditional grid.

Page 17 takes place after Stel and Atan have crashed on the planet (fig. 5.4). Stel is trying to fix a vehicle to go exploring, while Atan is cooking spaghetti. Giraud omits the background in all but the first and last panels and occupies the middle of the page with four panels that work as a series. The orthogonal point of view, at eye level and the attention to minute variations contrast sharply with the radical disjunctions and the spectacular framings commonly associated with his work. The sparse composition of the panels focuses attention on one or two subjects, near the center of the frame or symmetrically arranged.

This process of paring down applies to the drawing line itself. The accessories used by Atan in the first panel are drawn in simple outlines, designed for flat colors, with minimal embellishment. They function as indexes to existing objects and concepts, not as individuated instances thereof. In the same panel, Atan's face is drawn as a precise outline, with minute inflections indicating the jaw, the chin, and the cheek and a total of six nib marks to suggest their features. The same principle of economy runs through every object on the page, with textures and features omitted or reduced to a minimum. The nib lines maintain an almost constant width, though unlike the sleek production of the Hergé studio, the image incorporates tiny accidents, trembled details, and a reluctance to embrace the perfect geometry of the ruled line. The page also includes discordant details, such as the ink marks on the wall, in the back of the first panel, or the sudden irruption of volume on Atan's arm, in the foreground of the third panel. However, it illustrates Giraud's commitment to the clear line as a design choice reflecting a philosophy.

By the time of the second album in the series, *The Gardens of Edena* (1988), he had broken with Iso-Zen, yet the series remained driven by mystical concerns. The original story, though open-ended,

Fig. 5.4. Jean Giraud, as Moebius, *Epic Graphic Novel Moebius 1: Upon a Star*, 1987 17.

had been intended as one shot, but the series became retitled as "The World of Edena," promising both a continuation of the various Edena projects launched with Appel-Guéry and a potential biblical tale. Atan and Stel are transported to a lush, Edenic planet, until eating an apple leads to gender differentiation, sexual violence, and separation. In the final pages of the story, a mysterious character named Maître Burg (a near anagram for Grubert) leads Stel into a dreamlike episode, during which he makes love to Atan—now Atana—before a dream monster assaults them.

As with the previous volume, most of *The Gardens of Edena* was created quickly—the first twenty-five pages were written and drawn in less than a month, while Giraud was in Tokyo waiting for the production of a Little Nemo animated movie to move forward (Giraud and Sadoul 2021, 96–97). Thematically and graphically, it starts very much like the first volume, though lines are slightly sketchier, scratchier, perhaps betraying the haste of the execution. The natural environment, such as the orchard in which the heroes find sustenance, also leads to a form of controlled proliferation: trees, bushes, and grass are prominent in the narrative, and rendered via abundant but orderly nib marks. At the midpoint of the story, a star shape in the sky surrounded by fairylike ethereal beings connects the work closely to Giraud's other Iso-Zen-inspired output. It also signals the end of the brief experiment with a strict clear line. Soon afterward, a freer form of drawing creeps back into the book, as the heroes move from the neat garden to a jungle and then a desert. The physical transformations and the sexual differentiation they undergo after consuming the forbidden fruits translate graphically into more distinctive faces and body. Stel's eyebrows cease being a simple line, hatching delineates the volume of his limbs, and as he enters the desert, some brushstrokes complement the nib. Discussing the volume with Numa Sadoul in 1988, Giraud acknowledged this return to a more familiar style: "I was very interested in the notion of a drawing that would be purely objective. But I see now that I have failed on that level: it is impossible, it has to be a myth. I do not regret trying; I have drawn useful lessons from the attempt" (Sadoul and Giraud 2021, 196).

In the subsequent discussion, he further specifies that he was nevertheless embracing a nuanced approach to storytelling, tending toward a pared-down line and moderating "effects" in favor of subtlety and empathy. Describing the graphic shift at the midpoint of the volume, he adds that the artist turns out to be the real hero of the story: the characters recover their sensuality as the author rediscovers the sensual pleasure of drawing. Since *The Gardens of Edena* works in part as a diary (2021, 195), this transition between page 24 and page 25 can rightfully be read as concluding his attempts to create art entirely in the service of a mystical philosophy. The rest of the series, five volumes, with the last one published in 2001, does not resemble earlier Moebius works, but it does not attempt to resurrect the temptation of "sacred art" either, and draws from Franquin as well as from Hergé. Giraud also abandoned the pseudonym *Jean Gir*, though the later phase of his career led to another attempt at convergence between his personas.

Blueberry

In spite of these profound transformations, Giraud continued working on Blueberry during the decade. After the mid-1970s break, which allowed Moebius to flourish, the series resumed publishing in 1979 with *Broken Nose*, serialized in *Super-As* and *Métal Hurlant*, then published as an album in 1980. Fittingly, it portrays a reborn Blueberry, now firmly on the side of Native Americans under the adopted name of *Tsi-Na-Pah*, who helps the Navajos fend off the US Army and escape the barren reservation in which they had been parked.

The early pages of the album include some of the most elaborate images in the series, with fluid landscapes resembling Moebius's alien worlds more than the lush rock faces of the earlier albums.

Complex layouts with novel effects—such as contoured faces superimposed on traditional panels—also provide evidence that he was exploring new narrative possibilities. While he was on the verge of his pivot toward sparseness as Moebius, these pages match the elaborateness of his celebrated early-1970s work. *Broken Nose* demonstrates the permeability between Gir and Moebius, while serving as a symbol of their historical decoupling.

These early pages proved so labor intensive as to be unsustainable in the long run. Giraud addressed the issue in two ways. The first was adopting a slightly more economical register in subsequent albums. The second was to rely on assistants, putting him in a position not unlike that of Jijé and Jerry Spring, twenty years earlier. Colin Wilson helped him finish *The End of the Trail* (*Le bout de la piste*, 1986), and before that, Michel Rouge worked as an inker on roughly half of *The Long March* (*La longue marche*, 1980), with Giraud seriously contemplating handing over the series to him (Sadoul and Giraud 2021, 126–27). In 1985, he also approved the creation of a spin-off series chronicling Blueberry's youth. Technically, the series had been launched ten years before, when Dargaud reprinted in the album format the small-format short stories that Charlier and Giraud had produced in the late 1960s for *Pilote Super Pocket*. These reprints spanned three albums, covering the hiatus in the series' publication. However, the 1985 story, *Les Démons du Missouri* (which remains untranslated), drawn by Colin Wilson under Giraud's supervision, presented new material and represented an attempt at expanding and consolidating the brand beyond its original creators. As part of this expansion, a well-received *Blueberry* videogame was produced by French publisher Coktel Vision (1987), and a film project was in discussion, before collapsing around 1986.

Thus, even as he was producing meticulously crafted albums, Giraud was accepting, even embracing, a more distant relation to the character. What had been his signature work, almost consubstantial with his career, had become one piece of an increasingly diverse portfolio, though still a lucrative one.

This distance from the series throughout the 1980s might also stem from its chaotic publishing history. As indicated above, *Broken Nose* appeared simultaneously in *Métal Hurlant*, targeting teenagers and young adults, and in *Super-As*, with a much younger readership. The following albums were published in *Super-As* again, then in *L'Écho des Savanes* (for adults), in *Spirou* (for children), in the center-leftist daily *Libération*, and so on. In truth, though pre-published in various outlets, the series was by then conceived for the album format, reflecting a broader shift within the industry. Instead of creating the story specifically for a magazine, Giraud and Charlier broke up existing material into long episodes, befitting the monthly publication schedule. Dargaud published *Broken Nose* in 1980—redoing the colors to keep them in line with previous albums—then the series moved to Fleurus, Hachette, Novedi, and Alpen, five different publishers over the course of six albums, between 1980 and 1990.[5]

Blueberry was a typical successful series in the 1960s, serialized in a high-profile magazine and then somewhat hesitantly republished in album form. By the early 1980s, it was still a fairly typical popular series, now centered on the book world, with each album constituting one episode in a long-running serial narrative.

The Moebius Brand

In his self-discourses, Giraud did not shy away from money concerns: he never claimed to practice art for art's sake and insisted on adequate compensation for his talent. He had entered the industry at a time when money was the only mode of recognition available to authors, and he openly pursued a stable income, even when willing to gamble some of his capital on a venture like *Métal Hurlant*. His use of the Moebius name for advertising concerns such as Eram, Alice, and Citroën fits this approach and serves as a reminder that many French comics creators, from Mandryka to Greg, also pursued this type of lucrative side projects.

Giraud differed from his peers in that he also sought to commodify his original work, cultivating a Moebius brand that relied upon and amplified his status as a singular artist, a genius.

This commodification first took the form of art books. *Venise Céleste* (1984), *Starwatcher* (1986), and *Made in L.A.* (1988) are large, thick hardbacks, with gorgeous reproduction. The first two were published by Aedena, a publishing house he had cocreated with Jean Annestay and that published mostly his work, along with an eclectic and impressive selection of translations (Frank Miller, Daniel Torres, Massimo Mattioli, Tanino Liberatore, etc.) between 1983 and 1987. In 1984, after breaking with Iso-Zen, Giraud and his wife, Claudine, relocated to California and started their own company, Starwatcher, as a US counterpart to Aedena, which focused on selling portfolios and art prints. In early 1986, the Girauds enlisted the help of Jean-Marc and Randy Lofficier, who helped market the Moebius brand to comics publishers and who became shareholders in the society. With the help of John Workman, *Heavy Metal*'s former visual director, they helped convinced Marvel to reprint most of Giraud's work between 1987 and 1991 and to expand the Moebius brand.

The most visible result of this expansion was the two-issue miniseries *Silver Surfer: Parable* (1988), scripted by Stan Lee. The project was a quixotic one, an attempt to do a superhero comic book by embracing the perceived limits of these comics, in terms of size, graphic choices, and coloring. In later reprints and in subsequent comments, Giraud discussed the result as a disappointment. Further efforts to expand the brand included a spin-off of *The Airtight Garage* (1990–92), the creation of a connection between *Arzach* and "The Detour" (1987), a novelization of *Arzach* (2000), and an ambitious use of the Moebius name for various projects. Paradoxically, after a comparatively fallow decade in the 1980s, Giraud was at the peak of his fame in the United States in the late 1980s, collaborating with Stan Lee and receiving casual praise from Harvey Kurtzman himself (Kurtzman, Brod, and Bisceglia 1988, 20).

Giraud, however, went back to France in 1989, separated from Claudine and lived with Isabelle Champeval, whom he had met in 1984. They got married in 1995 and had two children, Raphaël and Nausicaä, in 1989 and 1995, respectively. The relationship with the Lofficiers gradually soured in the course of the decade, culminating in the litigious dissolution of the company between 2000 and 2003. Meanwhile, Jean and Isabelle Giraud created a new structure in 1998, named Stardom/Moebius, then shortened to Moebius Production, which continues to this day. From 1985 to his death, Giraud thus sought to control his own commercial destiny, while continuing to work with traditional publishers for his traditional comics projects. In addition to embracing the image of an *exceptional* creator, he was thus creating the conditions to benefit fully from that exception. And in the early 1990s, after a decade of mysticism, he was finally ready to go back to his seminal 1970s work, *The Airtight Garage*.

Merging Personas and Becoming a Role Model

In 1989, Jean-Michel Charlier died, during the creation of the *Arizona Love*, the twenty-third Blueberry album. The story was supposed to inaugurate a new era for the character since the previous album, *The Last Card*, had concluded a narrative arc begun with *Chihuahua Pearl* in 1970. Having finally recovered his honor, Blueberry decides to pursue Pearl, his true love, and to disrupt her planned wedding to a rich but boring landowner.

Giraud finished the album on his own after Charlier's death. He deviated from the planned outline and changed the ending into a bittersweet one (Giraud and Sadoul 2021, 163–64). After a decade of brand expansion, he found himself as the sole author of the series, and even though contractual disputes emerged with Charlier's son about the existing portfolio, he could finally play with the main series as he pleased. After a five-year pause, he started the final phase of the saga, reframing it drastically and making it an emblem of his late work.

The Man from Ciguri, the Impossible Sequel

That pivotal period of the early 1990s was also defined by an unexpected failure. His US renaissance had created a renewed interest for the seminal Moebius works. In addition to Marvel, Dark Horse, Byron Preiss, and even Penthouse Comics published or republished his work, spreading the gospel and fueling enthusiasm for the comics he had created before his Iso-Zen-inspired asceticism. The publication of Ōtomo's *Akira* (1988–96), for which he wrote a preface, further demonstrated the range of his international influence.

In 1992, Dark Horse's anthology of international comics, *Cheval Noir* (1989–94), began publishing *The Man from Ciguri*, the sequel to *The Airtight Garage*. Reprints and translations create new context, and in this case, US readers went through a drastically compressed version of Giraud's career. In France, *The Garage* had been initially published in album form in 1979, but it was only collected in English by Epic in 1987, in color and with a new translation by the Lofficiers. *The Man from Ciguri* thus appeared in the United States as a direct continuation of the first book.

The Man from Ciguri embraces the mode of serial publication and starts with a possibly ironic caption—"later"—connecting it to its predecessor. The story picks up precisely where *The Garage* ended, with major Grubert stepping out of the subway and entering a mundane French city, still pursued by some of his foes. The book assumes familiarity with the first volume, barely bothering to reintroduce the protagonists or the stakes and assuming the convoluted cosmogony of the garage is accessible to the reader. In other words, it rests on the existence of dedicated Moebius fans—of late-1970s Moebius fans—eager for new layers of fabricated worlds.

Graphically, *The Man from Ciguri* bears traces of the developments in Moebius's art since *The Garage*. Grubert exists on the page a lanky silhouette with minimal textures and features. Similarly, the city in which he is wandering—while most of his foes and ally occupy a more typical science-fictional world—is mostly conjured through simple geometric shapes. However, the story also includes graphic throwbacks to Moebius's previous styles, with elaborate hatching and dots giving shape to fantastic visions. The first appearance of Grubert's ship, the *Ciguri* (p. 5), echoes both the framing and the rendering of two similar moments in *The Garage* (including one specially produced for the Epic version). Elsewhere yet, Giraud combines the clean outlines and simple texturing of his work on the World of Edena with a staggering profusion of details, especially in crowd scenes, which recall the fully realized environments of "The Long Tomorrow" or the early *Incal* pages. On several occasions (pp. 9–10, 12), pages and panels from *The Garage* are redrawn using techniques that differ from the original version, and some episodes include jarring graphic disconnects from panel to panel (fig. 6.1). All of this suggests that Giraud was trying to recapitulate his career as Moebius, revisiting styles and previous images, in addition to one of his most influential stories.

However, this flattened career overview failed to generate the same enthusiasm as its forerunner. Publication in *Cheval Noir* became sporadic and concluded in November 1993 (issue 41) with a hastily drawn episode, followed by an unspecific promise: "The Man from Ciguri will continue."

Taken together, the episodes published by Dark Horse amounted to only about thirty pages. In 1993 and 1994, Giraud continued working on the story and produced twenty more black-and-white pages, which remained unpublished at the time. The plan was to complete a thick volume of around one hundred black-and-white pages, recalling the format of the original *Garage*. However, Les Humanoïdes Associés opted to publish the work in a more traditional form, dividing it into two shorter color albums. For the first time perhaps, Giraud's work as Moebius became shaped by industrial standards against his expressed intent (Sadoul and Giraud 2021, 223; Trondheim and Giraud 1996, 6). In 1994, he added new episodes, redrew the final pages, and completed the planned first volume. However, disappointing sales led Humanoïdes to scrap the plans for the second one, and the remaining twenty-two pages were only published once afterward, in the fairly obscure *Moebius comic* (Caliber Press, six issues in 1996 and 1997), leaving the story unfinished.

Critical reception to *The Man from Ciguri* has been harsh. Mathias Wivel, writing in the *Comics Journal* in 2009 states bluntly: "It does not work. The fact that it is clearly scripted leaves attempts at evoking the improvisatory spirit of the original dead in the water, and the injection of yet another meta-thematic level in the form

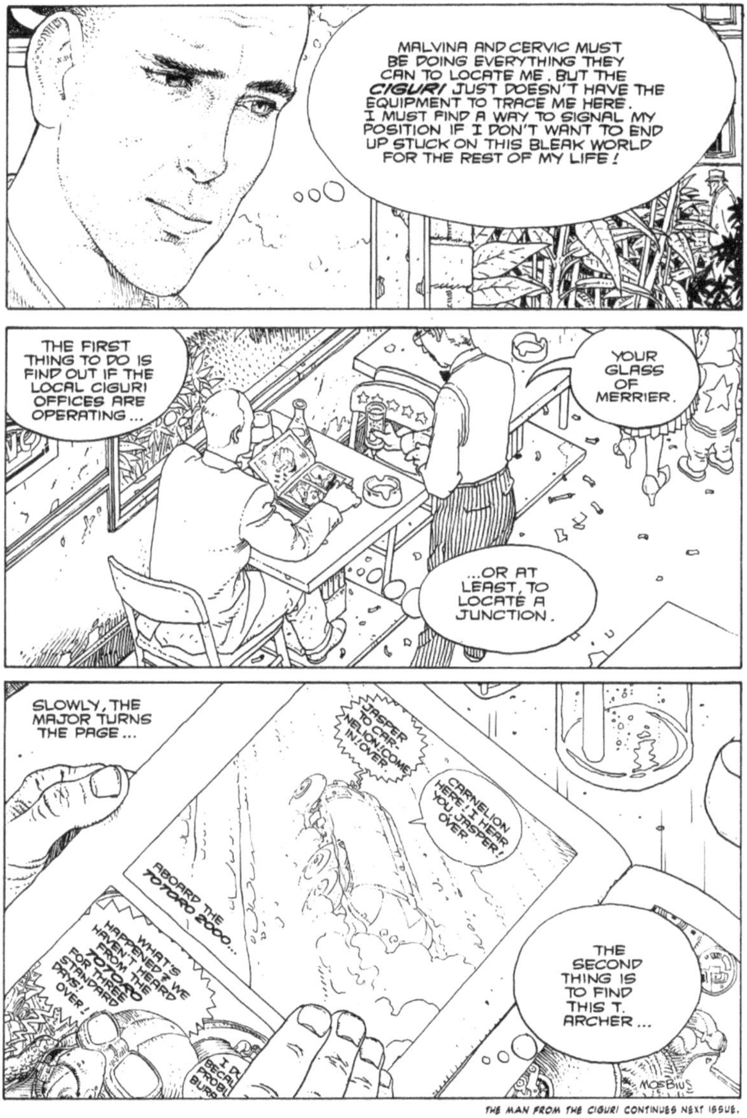

Fig. 6.1. Jean Giraud, as Moebius, *The Man from Ciguri*, *Cheval Noir*, issue 29, 1992.

of the artist's long-haired '70s alter ego from 'La Déviation' [. . .] only momentarily serves to distract from the feeling that we are witnessing a number of ineffable, wondrous concepts trotted out for an encore no one asked for" (Wivel 2009, 263).

The project of expanding *The Garage*, an improvised story, brought into passing coherence only by a deliberate decision in the final pages, was probably self-defeating and resulted in a critical and commercial failure. This may explain why Blueberry became the focus of Giraud's most sustained mainstream efforts in this final phase of his career and why his later attempts at autobiography did away with fiction almost entirely.

Mister Blueberry

Before reviving Blueberry on his own in 1995, Giraud carried on the expansion of the brand, with his own spin-off: Marshal Blueberry. Drawn by William Vance, whose style had been compared to his own early in their respective careers, the series was unremarkable, though it showed that Giraud could still write a fairly standard Western script, which he had not done since the 1960s. Blueberry's Youth also continued between 1990 and 1995, with four new albums, scripted or co-scripted by François Corteggiani, a prolific and classical writer.

Giraud's first solo album, *Mister Blueberry*, was published by Dargaud, the series' historical publisher. It featured new endpapers, a new coloring style (though the colorist, Florence Breton, had also worked on *Arizona Love*), and a new cover layout, which remained in use with slight variations for the next four albums. Together, these five episodes became identified as belonging to a Mister Blueberry cycle, distinct from the Charlier era. As early as 1974, Giraud had described the series as an "ego-comic," "drawn for its own sake" (Frémion 1974c, 86); after having envisioned abandoning the series in the mid-1980s (Charlier and Fuéri 1999, 36), Giraud made the character fully his own.

The five albums, published over ten years tell a complete story, culminating in the shootout at the OK Corral and lingering to examine its consequences on the main cast. Giraud had long described Blueberry as his alter ego, getting older and more grizzled over the years. In *Mister Blueberry*, this autobiographical reading offers a contrasted picture of his career in the late 1990s.

When the story begins, Blueberry has stepped away from this former life. Having long abandoned the army, he has also renounced his life as a gunslinger to become a poker player. He is back where the first page of the first album introduced him, before he was dragged to memorable adventures in Fort Navajo. While momentous events take shape around him, driven by a host of new characters, he refuses to commit, sticking to his game. Eventually, though, violence catches up with him, and he is pronounced dead, upon being shot by the son of a defeated poker player. The collapse of the hero figure continues in the next two albums—*Ombres sur Tombstone* (Shadows over Tombstone, 1997) and *Geronimo l'Apache* (Geronimo the Apache, 1999)—which Blueberry spends entirely in bed, telling stories, joking, flirting and recovering. Even after getting out of bed, he spends the final two albums, *OK Corral* (2003) and *Dust* (2005), as a staggering, wounded old man, on the sideline of the famous shootout.

Giraud resists the temptation to fully restore Blueberry, undercutting his redemption with humor and odd pacing choices, including abundant flashbacks, which run against any epic reading. In that sense, the Mister Blueberry albums are far removed from Charlier's ever-rebounding adventures and often appear deliberately contrarian when juxtaposed with the earlier albums. Without entirely relinquishing the Western genre, Giraud applied some of *The Airtight Garage*'s deconstructive verve to his longest-running character (while playing him straight in his script for the third Marshal Blueberry album in 2000).

The renewed influence of Moebius on Gir is also on display graphically, in particular through the use of caricature. Exaggerated and expressive features had been part of the series since the early albums (for instance in *The Lone Eagle*, the third story in the series), but these five albums use every opportunity to distend bodies and to tweak faces so that the cast of characters hover on the edge between realism and pure cartoons; in that sense, they echo *Angel Face*, the transitional album from 1975, drawn in the formative period of his Moebius identity.

Giraud's brushwork is more restrained than in previous albums, often eschewing bold strokes and lush textures in favor of a fluid but more controlled approach, which reduces the difference with more rigid drawing tools, like the nib or the rapidograph. From Moebius albums, such as the late *Incal* volumes, he also imports close-ups dominated by a thick contour line rather than by the details of the faces, calling attention to the drawing hand and the ink on the page, rather than to the texture of the storyworld. In some weaker passage, that sense of a shared world, which had defined the series up to that point, vanishes in backgroundless panels.

Additionally, Florence Breton, the colorist for the first three albums in this narrative arc, deviates from the earthen tones that had become the default approach to the series.[1] In addition to *Arizona Love*, she had worked with Giraud mostly as Moebius, on the third volume of the World of Edena, for instance. In *Mister Blueberry* and the next two albums, she introduces sharp greens and generally radiant colors, as well as a sustained modeling of faces through tones, though the last two albums of the series play down these changes. These innovations do not upend the aesthetic of the series, but they bring it closer to the flamboyant excesses of Moebius colors, whether done directly by Giraud or by others under his supervision.

After failing to recapture his earlier success as Moebius, Giraud thus offered a poignant recapitulation and synthesis of his career in the span of these five albums. As if echoing the ritual banquet in Astérix, his final Blueberry album, *Dust*, concludes with all the characters sitting at a round table and celebrating the end of their adventures. With a broad smile, Blueberry declares himself ruined, but alive, and ready to play again. While struggling to finish Mister Blueberry, Giraud equated the character's downfall with his own: "Blueberry had to get out of his depression, but for this to happen, I need to fight with him and to cure my own wounds" (Moebius 1999, 139). By the end of the story, Blueberry and Giraud appear rejuvenated—narratively and graphically—having overcome the crisis.

Blueberry is not, or not only, an autobiographical story. The resurrection of the hero and his will to go on in spite of everything also reflect the destiny of serial heroes, forever likely to go through one more episode, one more adventure. And while the series ends up on an optimistic note for its protagonist, it also displays the decline in Giraud's abilities. Faces and perspectives lose some of their sharpness; backgrounds are simplified or even dropped entirely. In the fourth album, *OK Corral* (2003), a wounded Blueberry stumbles and falls in the street, and poignantly, the page is almost devoid of backgrounds, with easy tricks (gradients, thick brush lines) barely hiding their absence. Critic Matt Seneca, writing about these albums expresses this state of his career concisely: this is "le maître à la fin," the master toward the end.

Final Moebius

The last Blueberry album was published in 2005, concluding the Mister Blueberry arc, shortly after the release of the long-awaited but poorly received movie adaptation by Jan Kounen (*Blueberry, l'expérience secrète*, 2004). Its spin off dedicated to the character's youth continued for a further eight albums, until 2015.

Meanwhile, as Moebius, Giraud collaborated on a new project with Alejandro Jodorowsky, a three-volume mystic farce entitled *Madwoman of the Sacred Heart* (1992–98). Set in a contemporary setting, the story follows the playfully sacrilegious adventures of a philosophy professor whose student turns out to be a reincarnation of the Virgin Mary. Though superficially ambitious, the tone is mostly silly and bawdy—complete with scatological gags—and turns into a South American adventure in the final volume. The first two books, published in a difficult period for Giraud (1992–93), display an art in constant flux, in which poorly executed panels contrast with finely detailed renditions of complex scenes, and in which the influence of Franquin and Hergé seem to be at war with each other. A neatly delineated, clear-line approach alternates with loosely sketched pages; realistic depictions turn into big foot caricatures from one page to another (see p. 27 in the second volume, for instance). The third volume, published after a five-year gap,[2] is no less silly but more internally consistent, with denser pages (four, five strips per page, while the other two books had three), and a wholesale embrace of caricature. In the final pages, Giraud seems to be channeling the plasticity of Jack Davis or Bill Elder's characters, with elongated limbs and hyperexpressive features, delineated in broad strokes and thick outlines.

In 2001, Giraud published his final contributions to his two defining science-fiction sagas. *Sra* concluded the World of Edena, seven years after the cliffhanger of the previous book, *Stel*. The series had evolved considerably since the first volume in the Iso-Zen period. *Stel*, in particular, had embraced textures, rocky landscapes, and detailed environments, to create a palpable, inhabitable secondary world in which the main character lived through adventures dominated by the laws of physics. *Sra*, by contrast, goes back to the sparse lines of the first two volumes, told in two or three vast panels per page. A few scenes feature spectacularly detailed environments but the focus is on the characters, drawn in simple outlines and vivid colors, while the reliance on mystical progression and dream states removes the necessity of building an internally consistent world. Unlike the three-volume *Madwoman of the Sacred Heart*, this is a controlled album, driven by a coherent esthetic. The series ends with Stel flying away to Edena in a red-and-white spaceship, the colors of Hergé's iconic rocket in *Tintin*, driven by Atana's virtual image. Though the overall narrative remains incomplete, a secondary character observes: "Something tells me we will not see this guy again anytime soon."

The same year, Giraud also returned to *The Incal*. Since the publication of the final volume in 1988, the series had proliferated. A sticker on the seventh printing of the first volume in 1998 claimed that the series had sold 1 million copies. It is unclear whether that figure accounted for the ancillary series, including a six-album prequel (*Avant l'Incal*, 1988–95) and three spin offs. Among these three, the eight-volume story, which centered on a family of space warriors, the metabarons (*The Saga of the Metabarons*, 1992–2003), with spectacular painted art by Argentinian artist Juan Gimenez,[3] had become a success in its own right. Expectations were therefore high when Giraud returned to the saga.

Après l'Incal follows the further adventures of John Difool and posits that the entirety of the first saga was a dream, haunting him. The story reboots the original, replaying some scenes, shifting others, and playing on the confused memories of the main characters and presumably of the readers. As such, its ambition falls short of the universe building in the original saga, instead offering a derivative rereading of its greatest hits and iconic images (the police station, Difool falling through the pits of the vertical city, etc.). The work is also disappointing graphically, in large part because of the coloring. Giraud worked with numerous colorists in the later part of his career, including Florence Breton and Scarlett Smulkovski, on both *Madwoman of the Sacred Heart* and Blueberry. He also did his own colors in a variety of cases (*Stel*, *Sra*, *OK Corral*) and fully embraced the possibilities offered by digital tools, including special effects such as gradients. In all of these cases, the works use bright colors, high contrast, and subordinate "realism" to legibility. By contrast, *Après l'Incal* was colored by the Studio Beltran, which specialized in metallic tones and ubiquitous modeling. The digital coloring and the special effects (gradients, clouds, grass, city lights, etc.) dominate the pages, drenching them in metallic greys and bright reds. Giraud's drawing, with bold outlines and few details, is a poor fit for this form of performative "realism." Like *The Man from Ciguri* a few years earlier, though for different reasons, *Après l'Incal* turned out to be a failure, according to everyone involved.

Puzzlingly, Les Humanoïdes Associés decided to reprint *The Incal* itself with the same coloring in 2003, before reverting to the original colors for subsequent editions. Jodorowsky later revisited the story of *Après l'Incal* with Mexican artist José Ladrönn, who redrew an altered version of the first volume and then completed the narrative as *Final Incal*, between 2008 and 2014.

The Moebius brand and persona were thus associated with a series of incomplete or disappointing works in the late 1990s and early 2000s, produced in collaboration with Jodorowsky or in attempts to embrace the serial conventions that early Moebius had railed against. From "The Detour" onward, he had described Moebius as his freer, more authentic alter ego, an improvisational personality. That approach was ill-suited for the compromises with industrial norms that he had pursued since the 1980s. In the beginning of the twenty-first century, he pushed back from these constraints and from the norms of popular fiction.

In 1999, he published *Moebius-Giraud, histoire de mon double*, his "autobiography without dates" (Moebius 1999, 7). The fragmented and incomplete narrative examines the Gir/Moebius duality almost as much as Giraud's personal life but contains a detailed account of his experience in Mexico in 1956, an initiation to jazz, sex, and drugs, and moving pages about his family and about Claudine, his first wife. The book also reaffirms the connection between his work and the economic circumstances presiding his creation: style, his and others, results from skills but also from market conditions (108) and from specific historical conditions (113). A few pages later, suggesting that all graphic artists share a filiation with da Vinci and Rembrandt (118), he includes the entirety of art history within this social and economic paradigm. Drawing may be transcendent, but "it is essential for a draftsman to be published, for it is only then that he really sees his drawings" (121). The only "geniuses" mentioned in the book are Harvey Kurtzman and Bill Elder, for their work on the early *Mad* (163). Best read in conjunction with Numa Sadoul's interviews, the book sheds a light on Giraud's worldview shortly before the twenty-first century, downplaying forgotten doctrines (five years of Iso-Zen are covered in a page, while a few months' stay in New York warrants half a chapter), praising friends and masters, and hinting at new vulnerabilities. It reaffirms the central place of drawing in Giraud's life and self-perception, and as such foreshadows the autobiographical turn of his fiction as Moebius in the following decade.

The same year, his most spectacular book as Moebius since the 1970s came out in an unusual presentation: *40 Days Dans le Désert B*, a small black-and-white book in landscape format. Its seventy pages, printed at the size of the original art, present a succession of images in which a shamanic hooded figure meditates serenely in an ever-changing desert, before spontaneously combusting. The book was drawn with a rapidograph, without preliminary sketches and in a "totally spontaneous manner"; Giraud later described it as "the most interesting thing to come out of [his] pen" (Sadoul and Giraud 2021, 225).

In the title, *Désert B* is a pun on *désherber* (to weed) for the book was drawn to reflect on Giraud's abandoning his use of marijuana. As its bilingual title suggests, the book straddles many divides. It is at once fantastic and personal, illustrative and narrative, as the succession of full-page images construct a loose sequence, especially within the horizon of expectation set by his previous work. On the other hand, its format and its self-publication, through Stardom, then Moebius Production, sets it firmly apart from the mass-printed serialized narratives of the decade. Unlike many of the books Giraud had produced since the 1980s, alone or with Jodorowsky, *40 Days* does not seek to elucidate its mystery or to preach. On page 5, the shaman is facing a distant stranger who is wearing a costume emblazoned with a star, incorporating a motif running through the post-1970s Moebius work. On page 6 (fig. 6.2), however, the shaman and the stranger keep their place on the page, but the star is gone, and a host of new characters perform an erotic dance and ritual between them. Sensual bodies and further tiny mysteries—a dart-shaped animal, intertwined tentacles, rows of

Fig. 6.2. Jean Giraud, as Moebius, *40 Days dans le* Desert *B*, 1999, ill. 6.

living totems, tattoos, and cryptic body language—displace the crystalline enlightenment metaphors of the World of Edena or *The Incal*. A caption added in the later editions emphasizes the disjunction: "Arshamanic meditation is immediately demented, sexual and chaotic."

In a 1999 interview, on the occasion of an exhibit of his sketchbooks at the Cartier Foundation, Giraud stated that he was unwilling to ever print these "solitary pleasures" and defended the idea that they differed significantly from his comics works (Moebius and Vidal 1999, 38). A year later, he started drawing *Inside Moebius*, a sketchbook comic story, which he published in six volumes, from 2004 to 2010.

Inside Moebius echoes *40 Days* and takes place in the same setting, but it operates a dual shift. Graphically, it replaces spontaneous virtuosity with virtuoso spontaneity, and thematically, it turns a fiction processing autobiography into an autofiction. Each page in *40 Days* serves as a display of excess, world-building improvisations conjuring texture and weight down to the last rock, and accomplishing the same tour de force repeatedly around a set of motifs. Through virtuoso craft, it transmutes inventions into the illusion of perfect control. Conversely, in the early volumes of *Inside Moebius*, each page is a hasty scribble, an autographic line pointing to the hand of the artist and seeking to hold in its very crudeness what Rodolphe Töpffer called "the divine breath that cannot be measured or captured," (qtd. in Smolderen 2014, 28) with minimal evidence of a shared fictional world. As Giraud's avatar remarks upon entering a temple-like building: "This feels like a Moebius comics, only much less slick."[4] The desert is a fruitful locale for such explorations, allowing both the mineral verisimilitude of Blueberry's landscapes and minimalist figuration of an idea, reduced to a single line separating the ground from the sky. At the end of the first volume, Giraud's aging, balding avatar stumbles and struggles but manages to take flight over his desert, vanishing in a nearly empty page (fig. 6.3)—a tiny figure, and at the bottom of the panel, two lines hinting a row of dunes—over a scribbled inscription, "to be continued." In the printed volumes, simple digital colors reinforce the cohesiveness of the narrative sequence and help create chromatic intericonic links to his other works but do not overpower the simplicity of the line. Answering a questionnaire for the fanzine *Post Scriptum* in 1981, Giraud had indicated that his greatest fear was to "fall back to earth" (Giraud 1981, 22). Twenty years later, he defers that fear indefinitely, in the liminal space between volumes.

Inside Moebius serves as an expansion of Giraud's autobiographical impulse, and, as he later remarked, it revisits a strategy and a style he had first used for his drawn interview with Numa Sadoul, in 1975 (Sadoul and Giraud 2021, 234). Giraud's avatar, a balding, big-nosed representation, downplays his considerable personal charm—somewhat resembling Bill Murray's—to turn him into a stereotypical aging Frenchman, wearing a bright yellow T-shirt as a uniform. That Giraud reflects on his limitations and failing creative powers, illustrated by his trouble writing a script for Blueberry. He soon gets to meet a younger version of himself—the cannabis-smoking, long-haired 1975 Giraud—then his iconic characters,

Fig. 6.3. Jean Giraud, as Moebius, *Inside Moebius*, 2001, final page of volume 1.

Blueberry, Geronimo, the Major, Malvina, the pterodactyl rider from *Arzach*, Stel, Atana, and other minor figures. Those characters serve as a Greek chorus, looking for their creator and seeking to understand his thought process and his diminishing creative power. Blueberry, in particular, tries to get Giraud/Moebius to finally write the final volumes of Mister Blueberry, forever reminding his creator that his series makes money, unlike all of his other side projects. Some of their interactions are playful or absurd, relying on the pleasure of unlikely meetings: Stel and Blueberry in a canyon, Arzach drinking tea with the major and revealing his "true form" as a colored abstraction. In other cases, the characters wonder whether their creator has gone mad or is depressed. In volume 2 (drawn in 2001, published in 2006), a cryptic scene acknowledges his deteriorating physical condition, as faceless angels pump out "the blackness" filling his body, the cancer that eventually killed him.

Inside Moebius plays with personas. Even the putative author figure—the aging Giraud in his yellow T-shirt—repeatedly acknowledges that he is a representation rather than a direct manifestation of the author. Its dialogues undermine claims to immediacy or authenticity. However, while the conclusions may be jocular, the recurring themes coursing through the nearly seven hundred pages of the six published volumes mesh with what we can gather of Giraud's preoccupations at the time. For instance, visiting his "ego bunker" with his younger alter ego, he stumbles in front of a locked door leading to "art," scratched with fingernails, and remarks that the door is especially hard to open since it has no lock. Like his characters, Giraud keeps crossing thresholds, falling and mutating, hoping to be able to fly again. Starting with the third volume, Giraud also encounters an even younger self, himself at the age of seven (vol. 3, 103). The moment inverts the strategy of self-representation he had used in "The Repairmen," in which Stel met an unnamed avatar of the author and fixed his submarine. That story integrated an autobiographical shard within a fictional world. In *Inside Moebius*, the autobiographical shards are so numerous that they constantly protrude through the thin veneer of improvised fiction.

In a retrospective look on Giraud's career, Matthias Wivel observes his use of a "star-system" resembling Tezuka's, in which characters reappear across series, playing different roles (Wivel 2009, 262), a theme also developed by Michael Moorcock in his Jerry Cornelius novels, which inspired *The Airtight Garage*. In *Inside Moebius*, this star system serves as the backdrop to the underground comix Giraud never really produced during the 1970s, a rich tapestry of generic and personal tropes against which his personal anxieties and enthusiasm play out. He notably claims this delayed filiation with the underground in an episode during which a regressive Giraud avatar suckles on the massive breasts of a smiling and buxom nurse, leading the major to decamp in a panel mirroring Robert Crumb's "Keep on truckin'" image.

The result is bittersweet. The recurring comments about Giraud's diminishing ability to draw function as more than jokes. Yet, again and again, Giraud takes flight. In the final page of the final volume, drawn in 2009 and published the following year, the 1970s version of himself contemplates a mask of his other self but puts it back before walking away. The increasing refinement of the art also speaks against any hint of resignation. Starting with volume 3, the temptation of the elaborate drawing becomes manifest. Looking for the authors, his main characters arrive and marvel at a full-page drawing of the luxury palace, as Arzach comments: "I can't imagine the royalties it has taken to create such an environment" (vol. 3, 40). They suspect that there may be a script after all—and a degree of consistency does in creep in at this point—but Giraud appears mostly interested in putting his drawing skills to use. The desert may still appear as two lines (with purple clouds, for "purple clouds always look good" [vol. 3, 15]), but it also transmutes, from page to page, into a more elaborate version of itself (vol. 3, 91), putting Blueberry in a familiarly realized setting for instance (vol. 3, 43). By volume 5 (drawn in 2004, published in 2008), the refinement of the art far exceeds that lavished on conventional albums such as *The Madwoman of the Sacred Heart*. The minimalist final page of the first volume is repeated, redrawn, in even more elaborate versions in the course of the six volumes. After playing with Töpferrian scribbles to capture the free movement of the lively hand, Giraud's self-examination leads him to draw instead to the utmost of his ability.

Inside Moebius also offers insight on the ambiguous role of the publishing process in Giraud's late career and the tension between control and diffusion. The gap between drawing and publication for the early volumes confirm that they may not have been intended for publication (Sadoul and Giraud 2021, 235), but the reader is present early on: "I may shock sensitive readers!" / "Who cares? Here, precisely, we don't give a damn about the reader." (vol. 2). By the beginning of volume 4, the Giraud avatar observes that he only tolerates himself and his readers in his desert (vol. 4, 8), and the spectacular pages that open volume 5 present a desert full of advertisements for other Moebius works, as Malvina ironically comments: "The album sales are about to soar!" (vol. 5, 26). Being published, being seen, being read is an integral part of the project and a major thematic concern throughout. As in "The Detour," this is a professional autobiography, centering on Giraud as an author and leaving out almost entirely the rest of his life. The books themselves echo this ambiguity. Giraud self-published them as handsome hardbacks in the typical graphic novel format, retailing for the equally typical price of €20 (the same size and price point as the French edition of *Fun Home* in 2006, for instance). However, the limited print runs of thirty-five hundred copies made the book hard to find and rapidly expensive. The back covers prominently display a "first printing" mention, targeting collectors more than readers. The complete 2016 complete collection with a print run of four thousand itself became hard to find and expensive, though a 2023 reprint has broadened its accessibility.

Final Major, final Arzak

This ambiguous relation to commerce is reflected in the other products sold by Moebius Production, including signed limited prints, art portfolios, and collaborations with luxury brand Hermès in 2010. It is also well expressed in the final appearance of two of his defining characters, the Major, and Arzach/Arzak, in 2008 and 2010, respectively.

After the failure of *The Man from Ciguri*, Giraud continued playing with the character of the Major, both in *Inside Moebius* and in sketchbooks. Some of these works were reproduced at sketchbook size in 2009 in *Le Major*, which functions as an alternate take on *Inside Moebius* and is also set in Desert B, centering on the character rather than his creator. For instance, the desert is initially said to be the Major's instead of Moebius's, and Grubert also goes through some *Inside Moebius*'s key motifs: locked in a box, falling and hitting the ground in a spectacular explosion,[5] playing around while suspended in the air. Giraud once more incorporates bedephile intertextuality, with two characters named Raoul et Gaston—the French translation of Lyman Young's comic strip, *Tim Tyler's Luck*—and revisits his own work, in a story haunted by the image of the spiral. While *The Airtight Garage* was an attempt at inscribing improvisation within the broad norms of adventure comics, *Le Major* attempts no such reconciliation. Moebius describes it as "utterly unstructured" in his introduction, drawing without underlying pencils and without a specific plan, relishing "poetic power play(s) made under the incredulous gaze of the powerless reader." The book incorporates major disjunctions within the narrative and also in the production process, with early pages produced in 1997 and then in 2001—contemporary with the beginning of *Inside Moebius*—then a mix of pages produced between 2006 and 2009, including contributions from family members and other comics artists (Cadelo, Loustal, Mattotti, etc.). The original print run appears to have been a mere one thousand copies, indicating a very narrow target, even by the standard of these late works.

By contrast, *Le Chasseur déprime* (again a pun, translatable as "the hunter is depressed" but sounding like the French for "bounty hunter"), published in 2008, functions as a more straightforward continuation of Grubert's adventures, as seen in *The Airtight Garage* and *The Man from Ciguri*, though it does not attempt to fill the gap left by the unpublished second half of the latter. A fifty-two-page black-and-white softcover album, it differs both from the small *Inside Moebius* and *Le Major* and from the more luxurious colored hardbacks of Giraud's mainstream twenty-first-century album. Like *Le Major*, this is a composite work, organized around new pages but incorporating a number of preexisting passages, some of which date back to 1998. No effort is made to hide this construction, which results in changing panel borders, balloons, and lettering, sometimes digitally overlaid on existing images (fig. 6.4, but also p. 24, for instance). The 1998 pages describe a depressed major, fed up with the airtight garage and misunderstood by all, much like Giraud at the beginning of *Inside Moebius*. Tasked with hunting himself, Grubert instead embarks in an exploration of nested dreams, under the guidance of a *survireuse* (oversteer), who resembles Giraud's wife, Isabelle. These dreams—a trap set by his foes, as in the later volumes of the World of Edena—result in transformations and metamorphoses, not unlike those of *40 Days in the Désert B*. As in *The Airtight Garage*, pseudo summaries introduce each chapter, and the pulpish plot propels the book, driving the assemblage of disparate images and forcing them into a semblance of narrative. In a perceptive review of the book, Martin Legoux, suggests that it functions as a museum of Giraud's art, playing not as a conflation of various genres but as an overt index of his own graphic possibilities, from the mid-1990s to the late 2010s (Legoux 2008), a point also made by Matthias Wivel (2012). The assemblage implies that the story is no longer improvised, but plays out a selection of previous hits—the desert, the nested worlds, the weird rituals—from which late, striking images, such as a host of giant and threatening rabbits, can be conjured. A promised sequel did not happen.

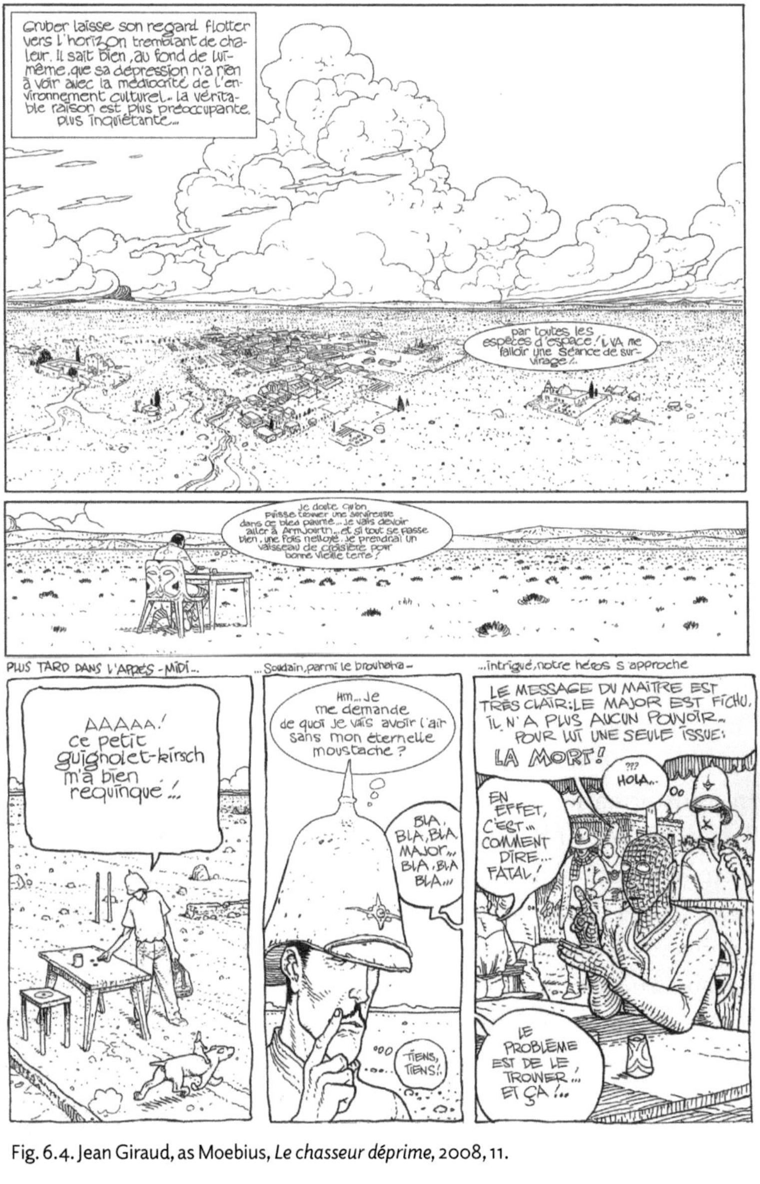

Fig. 6.4. Jean Giraud, as Moebius, *Le chasseur déprime*, 2008, 11.

The next year, Giraud published his final album, his most mainstream Moebius work since *Après l'Incal*. Nearly ten years after resurrecting the pterodactyl rider from *Arzach* in *Inside Moebius*, Giraud returned to the character in a large, color hardback, published in a coproduction between Moebius Production and Glénat, *Arzak l'Arpenteur* ("Arzak, the Surveyor," untranslated). Drawn using digital tools—like the later volumes of *Inside Moebius*—the book does not entirely escape the feeling of collage that permeates *Le Major déprime*. The balloons, created using regular shapes and with digital typefaces, do not mesh with the rest of the drawings and sometimes exhibit curious mistakes, such as variable interline spacing. Conversely, the exuberant digital colors, including vivid gradients in the gutters, bring a degree of unity to the book.

The unfinished story brings together shades of *Star Wars* (a princess on the run, dueling spaceships), *Time Masters* (a young boy, clinging to the comfort of his machine) and a desert in which the *Arabian Nights* intersect with the Western. Those disparate elements remain apart in that first and only volume, as Arzak himself wanders through the story with vague official responsibilities. With the exception of *Après l'Incal* and his volume of XIII, Giraud's twenty-first-century projects interlock and overlap, and this version of Arzak resembles the talkative character seen in *Inside Moebius*, more than its simpler, silent 1970s prototype. The first half of the book replays several spectacular scenes from that prototype, but in the second half, Arzak steps down from his pterodactyl, and his most striking skill lies in his ability to wait patiently in front of a tower. As late as 1999, Giraud defined the Moebius style as "mobility against immobility," a perpetual search for ecstasy (Moebius 1999, 167). A decade later, faced with declining motor skills and eyesight, Giraud emphasizes small joys and acts of resilience instead, in Blueberry, Grubert, Arzak, and his own drawing. In *Arzak l'Arpenteur*, he renders most of the traditional science-fictional elements in thick, simple lines, but his deserts and canyons still brim with details and nuances, conveying the power of the hand in motion, conjuring the remaining shreds of that vanishing ecstasy.

In Mister Blueberry, *Le Chasseur déprime*, and here, his characters are brought down, they grow old, weary, and wounded, hovering on thresholds. Yet, none of them dies, none of them crosses the threshold to achieve closure. Giraud's inability to conclude these series, but also the World of Edena and *Après l'Incal*, defer that closure indefinitely. As in the time of *Métal Hurlant*, the final "to be continued" reads "as a promise, primarily to [himself]" (Moebius 1999, 158).

In a poignant afterword to the color version of *Arzak l'Arpenteur*—a limited, silent version in grey tones was sold in late 2009—Giraud observes: "As to me, I now need more than a mere drawing, flowing from and insouciant pen on the corner of a table, to stumble unto a universe as rich and vast as that of Arzak" (Moebius 2010, 68).

Arzak l'Arpenteur represents a final effort to recapture through hard work and digital tools the carefree invention of his major works from the 1970s. The new adventures recapitulate and revisit that past, before settling in the syncretic twilight of the Desert B. It was his final published album.

A Decade-Long Celebration

Giraud spent the first decade of the twenty-first century recapitulating, revising, and curating his own career. Les Humanoïdes Associés followed suit in 2010 with a massive volume reprinting the stories they had the rights to, under a title harkening back to the early 1980s collection. However, *Moebius Oeuvres-Les Années Métal Hurlant* only included a portion of his work, excluding his production as Gir as well as most of his output after 1982.

Starting in the late 1990s, a series of museum exhibits offered their own views of his career, beyond the rigid borders of publishers' rights. There had been Giraud and Moebius exhibits before, but from Venice to Tokyo and Paris, these major shows multiplied after the late 1990s, in a self-reinforcing feedback loop. The discourse of genius runs through these exhibitions. The catalog for the 1997–98 *Moebius: Visioni de fine Millenio* in Milan compares him to Michelangelo, Dante, and Pascal (Giraud 1997). In 2000, the exhibition held in the comics museum in Angoulême, the CIBDI, was entitled *Trait de génie* (stroke of genius), and the subsequent catalog endeavored to justify this designation in the writing of comics scholars such as Thierry Groensteen and Thierry Smolderen (Groensteen and Ciment 2000).

By their very nature, such exhibits isolate the chosen artist from its milieu, elevating him and often invisibilizing the collective institutions through which his work was disseminated—*Métal Hurlant* has its own mythology and is often name checked in these shows, but *Pilote* rarely is. For instance, the 2005 exhibition at the Musée de la monnaie, in Paris, *Giraud/Moebius & Hayao Miyazaki* abstracted both creators from their respective setting to foreground their creative connection. Miyazaki was reportedly reluctant to be singled out from the structure of Studio Ghibli, and in fact, according to a reviewer, some visitors went through the exhibition thinking that Miyazaki worked by himself on his movies (Michaut 2019). Giraud's work was less reliant on collective labor, but as I hope to have demonstrated, it can hardly be abstracted from the broader environment of comics publishing. Regardless, both men were duly celebrated in the catalog as "great geniuses" (Valembois 2004, n.p.).

During this long decade, the press coverage for these exhibitions frequently embraced the framing of the genius as well (for instance Bernière 2001; Chapon 2004), though the most frequently mentioned works went back to the late 1970s and early 1980s. Giraud's influence on Hollywood, and to a lesser extent on manga, was by that time well established, and the legacy of *Alien*, *Blade Runner*, and *Akira* helped establish and maintain this reputation. The idea that had taken shape in comics circles in the mid-1970s was now repeated and adopted by mainstream institutions, in the course of a generational shift (early *Métal Hurlant* readers might be in their fifties by the early 2000s and well positioned to exert their cultural influence) and of a long process of legitimation of comics (Groensteen 2006; Lesage 2022).

The culmination of that decade-long celebration took place in 2010, at the prestigious Cartier Foundation for contemporary art, where Giraud had first exhibited his notebooks in 1999 (alongside Kubrick, Virilio, Tarkovski, and others), shortly before turning them into published works. The foundation was open to the avant-garde fringe of popular culture; its other 2010 exhibition was dedicated to filmmaker Takeshi Kitano, and it had hosted a selection of David Lynch's multimedia work in 2007, for instance. However, Giraud—or rather Moebius—was and remains the first comics artist to be exhibited there. Predictably, the foundation foregrounded his singularity within the field and his ability to move beyond its conventions: "An icon of incomparable stature in the world of comics, an inventor of extraordinary forms and a brilliant cartoonist, Moebius is an artist who goes beyond the traditional boundaries of the discipline. [. . .] Jean Giraud developed the unique style which he signed Moebius, publishing such groundbreaking works as *Arzach* (1976) and *Le Garage hermétique* (1979) that revolutionized the art of comics" (*Moebius Transe Forme* 2010).

Though entitled Moebius Transe Forme (Moebius trance form/transforms), the blockbuster exhibition, which ran for five months, offered a wide panorama of Giraud's career. It also included numerous looks at his process, including sketches, full stories, explanatory notes, color separation, and so on. Tightly coordinated by Giraud himself, it celebrated the entirety of his career and reflected his view on the importance of the published work, as opposed to the more Apollonian approach of the artist as a detached creator. While fully embracing the rhetoric of the genius, it made room for the craftsman, the draftsman, the comics creator. Notably, all of this is absent from the luxurious and now supremely expensive catalog published by Actes Sud. The huge hardback, weighing almost three pounds, includes gorgeous reproductions of works ranging from comics to abstract painting and three different types of papers and runs to more than three hundred pages. Yet, apart from three sketches, it contains no reference to the process nor to the books and magazines that most of the reproduced pages come from.

In response to the exhibition, *Beaux Arts* magazine, a fine art periodical that had made a habit of publishing comics-themed issues, ran an article by Belgian art critic and Hergé expert Pierre Sterckx purporting to explain "why Moebius is a comics genius." The cover of the magazine made it shorter: "Why Moebius Is a Genius." No question mark, and a status no longer in doubt. Even as he was publishing his final album, Giraud had reached that enviable status, far beyond the confines of the comics world.

On March 10, 2012, less than a year after the end of the exhibition, he died of a cancer diagnosed a decade earlier, having refused intrusive care that might have prolonged his life. Obituaries all over the world saluted his memory and offered a final recapitulation of a career he had been curating, exhibiting, and reexamining since the late 1990s. Tributes ranged from William Gibson, Katsuhiro Ōtomo, and Neil Gaiman to the French ministry of culture, from French newspapers to the *New York Times* and the Japanese *Asahi Shimbun*. Most of the acknowledged masters of comics, Hergé, Kirby, and Tezuka, died at a time when the medium was still struggling for recognition. When Giraud passed away, this stigma was long gone, and he was celebrated well beyond the comics world.

CHAPTER SEVEN

Conclusion: Afterlife

The Master

When Giraud died, comics creator Joann Sfar stated: "We have lost a father and a master" (Sfar 2012). Ten years earlier, in his drawn diaries, Sfar recounts having greeted Giraud—whom he always called Moebius—with a "Greetings, Master," to which Giraud replied, good-naturedly, "Oh, cut it off."

Giraud had influenced other artists since the 1970s, in France, Europe, and the rest of the world (for a tentative list, see Sadoul and Giraud 2021, 140–41). This influence had been felt primarily at the graphic level, here understood as encompassing technique, design choices, visual imagination, and in some cases, the science-fictional world building resulting from these elements. Comics creators as different as Milo Manara and Carla Speed McNeil, Frank Miller, and the Hernandez brothers have acknowledged this role, and French publishers of the 1980s actively sought new authors willing and able to produce passable imitations of his work. The emphasis on visual splendor is perhaps best expressed by Neil Gaiman's comment in an otherwise admiring tribute: "I finally read the Moebius stories in that *Metal Hurlant* when I was in my 20s, in translation, and discovered that they weren't actually brilliant stories. More like stream-of-consciousness art meets Ionesco absurdism. The literary depth and brilliance of the stories had all been in my head" (Gaiman 2012). *Heavy Metal* magazine deployed this rhetoric a lot in their early issues, positioning the stories primarily as visual demonstrations of virtuosity. Later testimonies suggest that this was even turned into an editorial policy when recruiting new artists (Rhodes 2012, Steve Bissette comment), though it was no longer supported by a discourse about cultural differences.

Giraud served as a different kind of role model for creators coming of age in the 1990s in France. These artists did admire his art, and Riad Sattouf, for instance, tried to imitate him early on (Sattouf 2020). However, Giraud served more as a perfect example of an attitude toward drawing and comics, a master admired not only for his work but also for his ethics.

The first significant meeting between Giraud and Lewis Trondheim did not go well in 1995 (Trondheim and Giraud 1996). Giraud was confusing—eventually rewriting the entire interview after the fact—and defended his publisher's choice to release *The Man from Ciguri* in color and in two volumes. Trondheim was among the creators of l'Association in 1990, the most visible independent publishing outlet seeking to redefine expectations about comics formats in France. Their author-driven approach embraced black-and-white books and atypical sizes, gesturing simultaneously toward the underground, the literary world, and the art world (Beaty 2007, 17–69). For instance, l'Association had published in 1992 *Lapinot et les Carottes de Patagonie*, a 500-page improvised picaresque narrative, echoing Giraud's creative process and unconventional length in *The Airtight Garage* (Minne 2012; Groensteen 2016). Giraud's "abdication" to commerce and the traditional format, which he had eschewed earlier in his career, seemed retrograde to Trondheim, in spite of his admiration for his work. Ironically, Trondheim himself soon found his own compromises with the traditional album format, as Dargaud (the original publisher of Blueberry) sought to enroll the creators associated with l'Association.

In spite of these fraught beginnings, the two creators became friends. In *Désoeuvré*, his 2005 comic about aging and decline among comics creators, Trondheim mentions Moebius as the most obvious exception to the rule that authors are exhausted after they turn sixty: "Obviously Moebius continues to do great stuff / He has always been curious and he has always renewed himself. / Moebius is the perfect counterexample for my theory" (Trondheim 2005, [9]). The same admiration is manifest in Sfar's account of his encounters with Giraud, as they argue about the value of the spontaneous gesture and the lively drawing, against the ideal of the perfected, complete illustration. They end up disagreeing, with Sfar decrying Giraud's "photographic" ideal, but Sfar nevertheless seeks and cherishes Giraud's worldview, returning several times to the topic in his drawn diary and showing the result to Giraud. In the summer of 2011, shortly before Giraud's death, Trondheim had started coordinating a collective series in *Le Journal de Spirou* chronicling the life of a fictional comics studio, *l'Atelier Mastodonte*. Published as weekly strips until 2018, the series brought together several *Spirou* creators, drawing themselves and each other, providing a kaleidoscopic view of a community of creators in the 2010s. Upon Giraud's death, *l'Atelier Mastodonte* ran a series of ten emotional strips, over three issues (*Le Journal de Spirou*, issue 3864–66, May 2012). Once more, they present Giraud as a "genius" but also as a kind creative partner, eagerly asking Yoann for a sketch or agreeing to draw a version of Trondheim's latest character based on a minimal description. Alfred describes Giraud's work as the reason why he started doing comics and Giraud himself as "comforting presence" that still surrounds the *Mastodonte* creators after his death. In this strip, and in another one by Julien Neel, the characters end up in the Desert B, dressed as Giraud's characters. Yoan, Alfred, Neel, and Trondheim are all successful creators, whose work spans independent graphic novels and transmedia popular series, yet they hold Giraud as model, and as continuing inspiration. In all these strips, he is not as a distant predecessor, but as an active and relevant peer, shaping these authors' own navigation of the compromises between individual expression and commercial success.

Though asymmetrical, the relationship was thus not sycophantic, with Trondheim frequently poking fun at Giraud's mysticism, his crystals, and the influence of Jodorowsky. In their accounts, Giraud appears interested in their points of view and in the validation afforded by this new generation. *Inside Moebius* reads as a continuation of the underground, but it was also published at a time when l'Association and other independent publishers (Cornelius, Ego comme X) had turned autobiographical and autofictional comics a distinct editorial segment. Trondheim's own *Approximativement* (six comic books in 1993–94, collected in 1995) shares a number of concerns and narrative options with *Inside Moebius*, for instance, and Guy Delisle—author of *Pyongyang* and *Jerusalem: Chronicles from the Holy City*—points out that a background character in *40 Days dans le Desert B* resembles Trondheim's self-representation from his autobiographical comics (Delisle 2010). More significantly, in *Inside Moebius*, Giraud hesitates between self-publication and going to l'Association, which would have placed him not only as a fellow traveler but also as a participant in that generational movement. Though both Giraud and the period in which l'Association appeared now recede in the past, this productive confluence has not gone away. As late as 2020, PLG published a collection of essays entitled *Plaidoyer pour les histoires en forme de champ de blé et de flamme d'allumette soufrée*, a call for "stories in the shape of an elephant, a cornfield or the flame of a match," quoting Giraud's famous editorial to *Métal Hurlant*, issue 4 and turning it into a program for future creators.

The publication by Sfar and Blain of a new Blueberry album in 2019, *Amertume Apache*, Apache bitterness, serve as an ambiguous coda for this convergence. Sfar describes the process as a continuation of their earlier exchanges. Giraud had considered asking Blain to draw the characters, in a "master and pupil" relationship but with a "mutual fascination." After Giraud's death, and on Dargaud's invitation, Sfar and Blain set out to do a "lively and relevant" album, but not a copy of the earlier work (qtd. in Tomblaine 2019). Throughout his interviews about the project, Sfar refers not to Moebius, but to Giraud, and even mentions the resemblance between Blain's art and Jijé's (Jean-Laurent Truc and

Sfar 2019), embracing the popular creator, the admirable craftsman more than the genius. Blain, a virtuoso himself, does not attempt to mimic Giraud—which he mentioned as a model as early as 2003 (qtd. in Beaty 2007, 201)—but takes him seriously, adjusting his own style to fulfill some of the expectations associated with the series. The album is part of a broader wave of continuations of popular series by new creative teams since the beginning of the twenty-first century, which has led to two different options: imitation (Astérix, Blake et Mortimer) or partial reinvention (Spirou, Valérian). *Amertume Apache* serves as a fine example of the latter, making use of its creators' cultural cachet and of their idiosyncrasies to keep a canonical series relevant. Even after his death, the legacy of Giraud's work remains determined by publishing trends and contractual demands, balancing out creative freedom. Meanwhile, this legacy has been challenged by new insights into his creative process.

Photo Reference, the Genius Reconsidered

Sfar's remark about Giraud's photographic ideal in 2003 took a new sting in the years following the publication of their exchanges. Giraud had never hidden his reliance on photographic reference for Blueberry, to ensure the credibility of all the requisite Western elements, and to further the continuity with the cinematic intertext. Horses, settings, faces, and entire covers thus came from various photographs, some of them meant to be recognized (Belmondo, Spencer Tracy, etc.) and others to remain invisible.

However, in the twenty-first century, fans and scholars tracked down many of the references underpinning his Moebius illustrations as well. Some of them, in *The Airtight Garage* for instance, had been obvious for years, but the extent of this use had not been known. In particular, Daniel Pizzoli has studied the role of photos collected in *The Human Form in Action and Repose* (Brodatz and Watson, 1966) throughout his career, from his science-fiction illustrations to his early *Métal Hurlant* stories, to much later ads and portfolios. Figures drawn after that influential reference book pop up in "The Detour" as well as in many of his illustrations. In other cases, the composition and figure work may be drawn from existing ads, in a process that resembles Lichtensteinian appropriation more than traditional reference work. Similarly, Giraud never acknowledged the influence of Poïvet's "Mix 315" on *Arzach*, which he described consistently as a product of his own imagination. There is little doubt that he had seen the story since he had drawn the cover to the issue in which "Mix 315" was printed, and even if he was not aware of the resemblance, it is unlikely that no one pointed it out afterward. Omitting his inspiration helped bolster his image as an innovator, but it certainly comes out as disingenuous.

A comment left on the *Comics Journal* website upon Giraud's passing sums up a widely shared disappointment about these revelations, which strike at the idea of Moebius as a combination of technical virtuosity and unfettered imagination: "At first I thought he was a fabulous artist, but lately I have found numerous examples of the photos which he swiped from. Many, many examples" (Thompson 2012, comment section). Digital tools and the availability of searchable image banks has made photo referencing a tempting and easy option for serialized comics, leading to widespread criticism of "swiping" and "tracing" and of the incongruous aesthetic such tools typically produce (a web search for these terms and *Greg Land* will reveal many examples). The late discovery of Giraud's reliance on these references thus took place in a context that differed markedly from his learning period with Jijé, during which compiling and maintaining a "morgue," a collection of references, was a common, useful, and mostly hidden practice for realistic artists.

Though extensive, even for some oddly banal images, Giraud's use of references was never systematic and appears to have occurred more in his stand-alone illustrations than in his comics. Discarding from his career the images directly inspired by existing art would leave intact his central claim to fame. At a more fundamental level, even these images are distinctly Giraud's, through a double process of rendering (redrawing, inking) and reconstruction (bringing the images in line with his visual grammar, though crystals, shapeshifting, or cold erotica). These images were not identified as swipes prior to the unearthing of their originals because they were also distinctly his, both in the lived traces of the drawing hand and in the imagination that reshaped them. In response to the comment in the *Comics Journal* obituary, another reader quoted Wallace Wood's famous maxim "Never draw anything you can copy, never copy anything you can trace, never trace anything you can cut out and paste up," suggesting that other noted artists had turned such inspiration into a method. But of course, Wood's motto was designed at a time when he was trying to meet deadlines and employing assistants to do so. The defense, while convincing, places Giraud in a world of deadlines and shortcuts, in the realm of virtuosos and master craftspeople, but perhaps not of geniuses.

Other reevaluations are likely to happen in the future, questioning for instance the representation of gender relations in his work. When Giraud started his professional career, comics magazines for boys, such as *Pilote*, had no female heroines and very few female characters overall. Accordingly, the first Blueberry story uses two contrasting archetypes, which define most of Giraud's female characters: the lovable young beauty and the stereotypical matron. In his later work, even as that crucial historical context receded, the young beauty tended to morph into a literal goddess, wielding sexuality as a mystical experience, but with little depth or agency of her own. In terms of graphic representations, Giraud aligned with his contemporaries: nakedness was introduced in Blueberry in *Arizona Love*, at a time when male-oriented eroticism had become acceptable, if not expected, in adult French comics. Similarly, the underground and *Métal Hurlant* had made a practice of displaying female bodies for the visual pleasure of their male readers. Giraud's work offers few egregious examples, displaying male and female full-frontal nudity in *Arzach* and "The Long Tomorrow," for instance, though the combination of female nudity and lack of agency offers a decidedly gendered eroticism. Carla Speed McNeil, noted author of *Finder*, offers a pointed critique of *The Gardens of Edena* in terms of gender roles, examining how these narrative and graphic choices intersect. She notes in particular the transformations that Atan/Atana undergoes after Edena's food awakens her feminine attributes. She is turned into an object of worship, a "goddess" without agency who needs to be rescued by the adventuring Stel. Meanwhile, Stel tries to rape her as they discover their new bodies, an attempt framed as clumsy, overeager affection (McNeil 2017). McNeil admires much of Giraud's work, as Moebius, whom she calls "a wizard, a visionary," but like Trondheim, she refuses monolithic praise, creating a clear hierarchy between his most successful books and his weaker or flawed attempts.

These discoveries have not affected noticeably the general discourse about Giraud in recent years—as recently as 2022, the new incarnation of *Les Cahiers de la bande dessinée* published an article claiming to show "why Moebius was a genius" (issue 18, April 2022). Yet his image as an absolute creator and a genius, a useful myth that he helped develop from the 1970s onward and that he may have believed, becomes harder to uphold as his career and compromises come into focus. Acknowledging his flaws, his failures, recognizing his blind spots and embarrassing silences does not take away from his best works, from his towering accomplishments in the field or from his constant ability to make light of his own pretensions. To be recognized and celebrated as a genius must have been a crowning achievement, but ten years on, the master craftsman is a richer, more complex, and probably more accurate description.

NOTES

CHAPTER ONE. INTRODUCTION

1. A selection of such images can be found on the Twitter account @midmoebius. These observations also derive from personal experience with various engines and a sustained examination of the Midjourney's discord servers. These engines could accidentally generate one perfect imitation, but the argument rests on the rarity of such occurrences.

2. I am indebted to the work of Charles Hatfield and Brannon Costello regarding the careers of Jack Kirby and Howard Chaykin, respectively.

CHAPTER TWO. JOURNEYMAN TO *PILOTE*

1. Fan histories of the medium have traditionally painted the 1954 Senate hearings and the implementation of the Comics Code as leading to a profound economic crisis in the field. This apocalyptic and monocausal reading has been challenged by recent scholarship. In addition to the now-accepted thesis that television competed for leisure time (Gabilliet 2010), Shawna Kidman offers a convincing examination of these effects and shows that the 1954 may have benefitted major publishers even as it led to the disappearance of smaller ones, consolidating the market as television was starting to threaten it. She also points out that the hearings compounded but did not create preexisting distribution issues which would have affected the market in any case. However, the code undeniably affected individual creators and companies and certainly precipitated a consolidation that might have happened in any case (Hajdu 2008; Kidman 2019).

2. Press regulation required children's publications to contain at least 10 percent of noncomic material, but in the late 1950s, magazines such as *Le Journal de Tintin* or the early *Pilote* devoted half their pages or less to comics material.

3. The title of the story is borrowed from the French title of Henry Hataway's movie *Wild Horse Mesa* (1932), but this is not an adaptation.

4. I am relying on the complete bibliography of Giraud's early work compiled by Patrick Bouster in *Hop!* 100 (December 2003)

5. Giraud mentions in an early interview with Numa Sadoul that he started working with Jijé in 1962, but their first work together was first serialized in March 1961. July 1960 is the date mentioned in the long interview Giraud gave to *Hop!* about his early career, and it appears to fit with the chronology of their collaboration (Giraud and Bouster 2003, 9), though early 1961 also seems plausible.

6. Somewhat quixotically, they attempted to translate the 1965 version of *Mad*, edited by Al Feldstein, though they later described that version as a betrayal of Kurtzman's vision.

7. Belmondo later became France's most popular actor, thanks to numerous light adventure films. In 1963, however, he was still associated with more radical filmmaking and the choice transgressed the boundaries of expected intermedial references at *Pilote* (Giraud and Ciment 2000).

8. Each of the albums exists in various versions, but Giraud made it a habit early on to number the pages in his stories and to include this numbering in the panels, leading to its inclusion across all versions and languages. Unless otherwise specified, when referring to specific pages from his work, I will rely on this numbering rather than on a specific edition.

9. Here and elsewhere, I will be using established English titles when they exist, and the most recent one in case of multiple translations.

CHAPTER THREE. ADULT COMICS AND THE COMING OF MOEBIUS

1. For instance, *Moebius Métamorphe*, a 2021 collection of essays published by Les Humanoïdes Associés, which contains Pizzoli's detailed use of the story, uses a blown-up panel of "The Detour" as its cover image.

2. In the translated edition published by Epic in 1990, the line is translated by Jean-Marc and Randy Lofficier as "déjà vu," which maintains the bilingual quality but inverts its value: the acknowledgment of foreign influence becomes a marker of Frenchness as exoticism. Ted Mann's 1981 translation in *Heavy Metal* magazine replaces the line with a cryptic "Gagg!" but makes up for this lost opportunity by changing the next line to a very appropriate "Now, this is Heavy Metal!"

3. Jean-Michel Charlier briefly became the editor-in-chief of *Le Nouveau Tintin* in 1976–77. The 1975 relaunch included both classic American strips and a number of former *Spirou* and *Pilote* luminaries, including Giraud.

CHAPTER FOUR. BECOMING AN INTERNATIONAL ARTIST

1. The communist *Pif Gadget* and *Le Journal de Mickey* had print runs of about 500,000 copies in the mid-1970s. *Pilote* had a print run of 168,000 copies in 1975 (Lesage 2014, 356, 1137).

2. Coincidentally, a somewhat similar parody—"Arnak," which sounds like the French for a swindle—appeared in the French fanzine *PLGPPUR*, issue 3, in the spring of 1979. The parallel confirms that Moebius was by that time an international star, inspiring fan creation on both sides of the Atlantic.

3. This is the *Heavy Metal* translation, which is closer to the French original than the 1987 translation for the Epic collection.

CHAPTER FIVE. A CELEBRATED ARTIST. A SHIFTING STYLE. A GENIUS?

1. The interview was reprinted in the Dutch prozine *Stripschrift* in 1972 (issues 39–40), introducing Giraud beyond francophone readers.

2. Ironically, Jean-Pierre Dionnet had already dubbed him "the father of the French underground comix" over a year earlier in the American fanzine *Graphic Story World*, in what was probably the first article devoted to him in the United States. The claim is, in any case, greatly exaggerated (Dionnet 1972, 15).

3. I have been unable to find a precise date for the publication of the book, but the fact that it was reviewed in *Charlie Mensuel* in December suggests that it was published during the second semester of 1974.

4. Bati, for his part, describes the project as an attempt by Giraud to set up a studio, in the aim of creating a cheap album, solely for the East European market. The interview fails to mention Iso-Zen and the specific circumstances it generated (Bati and Cudennec 2020).

5. The series subsequently moved back to Dargaud, its first publisher, which has since kept the albums in print.

CHAPTER SIX. MERGING PERSONAS AND BECOMING A ROLE MODEL

1. The serialized version of *Broken Nose* (1979) featured bold colors, but Dargaud had them redone by Evelyne Tran-Lé (who had worked notably on *The Lost Dutchman's Mine*) in a more muted style for the album version.

2. In the meantime, he had produced another book with Jodorowsky in 1994, *Angel Claws* (*Griffes d'Anges*), a pornographic illustrated story harkening back to their collaboration on *The Eyes of the Cat*.

3. Fittingly, Juan Gimenez had already worked in Moebius's footsteps in the early 1980s. He is credited as the concept artist for the "Harry Canyon" segment of the *Heavy Metal* movie (1981), directly inspired by "The Long Tomorrow."

4. In the Dark Horse US edition, Diana Schutz mistranslates this as "You'd think this was a Moebius comic . . . but not as clever."

5. Giraud first used that motif in "Absoluten calfeutrail" / "Free Fall," a 1977 story for *Métal Hurlant*, also improvised without preliminary pencil.

BIBLIOGRAPHY

Alessandrini, Marjorie, Jean Giraud, and Alejandro Jodorowsky. 1976. "Dune." *Rock & Folk*, May 1976.

Annestay, Jean. 1990. "Stel et Atan: Le monde d'Edena." In *Sur l'étoile*, 80–87. Le Monde d'Édena 1. Paris: Casterman.

Baetens, Jan, and Hugo Frey. 2015. *The Graphic Novel: An Introduction*. Cambridge Introductions to Literature. New York: Cambridge University Press.

Barber, Nicholas. 2019. "Is Jodorowsky's Dune the Greatest Film Never Made?" BBC.Com. March 14, 2019. https://www.bbc.com/culture/article/20190312-is-jodorowskys-dune-the-greatest-film-never-made.

Bati, Marc, and Brieuc Cudennec. 2020. "L'univers de Marc Bati." *Le Paratonnerre* (blog). February 10, 2020. http://leparatonnerre.fr/2020/02/10/lunivers-de-marc-bati/.

Baudry, Julien. 2022. "La Généralisation de La Bulle de Bande Dessinée En France Entre 1904 et 1940: Étude Systématique d'une Évolution de La Culture Visuelle." *Sociétés & Représentations* N° 53 (1): 81–102. https://doi.org/10.3917/sr.053.0081.

Baumann, Hask. 2007. *Moebius Redux: Une Vie En Images / Ein Leben in Bilder*. Deutschlan. http://www.imdb.de/title/tt1029340.

Beaty, Bart. 2007. *Unpopular Culture: Transforming the European Comic Book in the 1990s*. Studies in Book and Print Culture. Toronto; Buffalo: University of Toronto Press.

Beaty, Bart. 2012. *Comics versus Art*. Toronto; Buffalo: University of Toronto Press.

Beaty, Bart, and Benjamin Woo. 2016. *The Greatest Comic Book of All Time: Symbolic Capital and the Field of American Comic Books*. Palgrave Studies in Comics and Graphic Novels. New York: Palgrave Macmillan. https://doi.org/10.1057/978-1-137-53162-9.

Bernière, Vincent. 2001. "Moebius, Le Double Je." *M*, October 2001.

Blanchet, Evariste. 2006. "Métal Hurlant et Ses Frères." *Neuvième Art* 2.0. http://neuviemeart.citebd.org/spip.php?article131.

Boltanski, Luc. 1975. "La constitution du champ de la bande dessinée." *Actes de la recherche en sciences sociales* 1 (1): 37–59. https://doi.org/10.3406/arss.1975.2448.

Bonifer, Michael. 1982. *The Art of Tron*. New York: Simon & Schuster.

Cestac, Florence. 2007. *La Véritable Histoire de Futuropolis*. Paris: Dargaud.

Cestac, Florence. 2008. "Mettre l'auteur En Avant." *Neuvième Art* 14 (January): 64–75.

Chapon, B. 2004. "Miyazaki-Moebius, l'amitié fantastique." *20 minutes*, December 2, 2004. https://www.20minutes.fr/culture/40801-20041202-culture-miyazaki-moebius-l-amitie-fantastique.

Charlier, Philippe, and Jean-Pierre Fuéri. 1999. "Au Nom Du Père, Du Fils et de St Blueberry." *BoDoï*, November 1999.

Chavanne, Renaud. 2010. *Composition de La Bande Dessinée*. Montrouge: PLG. http://www.composition-de-la-bande-dessinee.net.

Chaykin, Howard. 2016. e-mail to the author.

Christin, Pierre, Enki Bilal, and Luc Pomerleau. 1989. "Called to Comics." *The Comics Journal*, May 1989.

Costello, Brannon. 2017. *Neon Visions: The Comics of Howard Chaykin*. Baton Rouge: Louisiana State University Press.

Crépin, Thierry. 1999. "Le Mythe d'un Front Commun." In *On Tue à Chaque Page!: La Loi de 1949 Sur Les Publications Destinées à La Jeunesse*, edited by Thierry Crepin and Thierry Groensteen, 43–51. Paris: [Angoulême]: Éd. du Temps Musée de la bande dessinée.

Crepin, Thierry, and Thierry Groensteen, eds. 1999. "Table Ronde." In *On Tue à Chaque Page!: La Loi de 1949 Sur Les Publications Destinées à La Jeunesse*, 217–33. Collection Dirigée Par Jean-Paul Gabilliet. Paris: [Angoulême]: Éd. du Temps Musée de la bande dessinée.

Dayez, Hugues, ed. 2002. *Blain / Blutch / David B. / de Crécy / Dupuy-Berberian / Guibert / Rabaté / Sfar: La Nouvelle Bande Dessinée. Entretiens Avec Hugues Dayez*. 2nd ed. Profession. Bruxelles: Niffle.

Debomy, Frédéric. 2020. *Plaidoyer pour les histoires en forme de champ de blé et de flamme d'allumette soufrée*. Mémoire vive 33. Montrouge: PLG.

Dejasse, Erwin, Tanguy Habrand, and Gert Meesters. 2011. *L'Association: Une Utopie Éditoriale et Esthétique*. Réflexions Faites. Bruxelles: Les Impressions Nouvelles.

Delisle, Guy. 2010. "Mœbius et Les Autres." *Guy Delisle* (blog). August 1, 2010. https://www.guydelisle.com/bd/moebius-et-les-autres/.

Delisle, Philippe, and Benoît Glaude. 2019. *Jijé: L'autre père de la BD franco-belge*. Mémoire vive 26. Montrouge: PLG.

Demange, Julie. 2017. "Bédéphilie." *Neuvième Art 2.0*, July 2017. http://neuviemeart.citebd.org/spip.php?article1169.

Di Manno, Yves. 1974. "Un Triomphe Du Baroque." *Schtroumpf: Les Cahiers de La Bande Dessinée*, 2nd semester, 1974.

Dionnet, Jean-Pierre. 1972. "The Many Lives of Jean Giraud." *Graphic Story World*, February 1972.

Druillet, Philippe, and David Alliot. 2014. *Delirium: Autoportrait*. Paris: les Arènes.

Druillet, Philippe, and Jean Léturgie. 1979. "Entretien Avec Philippe Druillet." *Schtroumpf: Les Cahiers de La Bande Dessinée*, 1979.

Druillet, Philippe, Christophe Quillien, and Jerry Frissen. 2022. "Entretien: Philippe Druillet." *Métal Hurlant*, Aout 2022.

Dutrey, Jacques. 2012. "Et Gir redevint Moebius . . . : genèse !" *BDZoom.com*. April 10, 2012. http://bdzoom.com/48006/patrimoine/et-gir-redevint-moebius-genese/.

Ecken, Claude. 2022. "L'essor d'un Journal." *Métal Hurlant*, Aout 2022.

Elder, Will, and Gary Groth. 2003. *Will Elder: The Mad Playboy of Art*. Fantagraphics.

Forceville, Charles. 2022. "Pictorial Runes." In *Key Terms in Comics Studies*, edited by Erin La Cour, Simon Grennan, and Rik Spanjers, 240–41. Palgrave Studies in Comics and Graphic Novels. Cham: Springer International. https://doi.org/10.1007/978-3-030-74974-3.

France-Soir. 1974. "Un Spécialiste Du Western," July 15, 1974.

Frémion, Yves. 1974a. "Les Petits-Miquets Font Les Grandes Oreilles." *Charlie Mensuel*, April 1974.

Frémion, Yves. 1974b. "Les Petits-Miquets Font Les Grandes Oreilles." *Charlie Mensuel*, May 1974.

Frémion, Yves. 1974c. "Les Petits-Miquets Font Les Grandes Oreilles." *Charlie Mensuel*, December 1974.

Gabilliet, Jean-Paul. 2010. *Of Comics and Men*. Jackson: University Press of Mississippi.

Gaiman, Neil. 2012. "Remembering Moebius." March 10, 2012. https://journal.neilgaiman.com/2012/03/remebering-moebius.html.

Gir. 1981. *Le Lac des émeraudes et autres récits*. Œuvres /Gir 1. Paris: Les Humanoïdes associés.

Giraud, Jean. 1973. "Entre-Giraud-Vue." *Falatoff*, June 1973.

Giraud, Jean. 1981. "Questionnaire." *Post Scriptum*, 1981.

Giraud, Jean. 1997. *Moebius: Visioni di fine millennio*. Lizard.

Giraud, Jean, and Patrick Bouster. 2003. "Entretien Avec Jean Giraud." *Hop!*, December 2003.

Giraud, Jean, and Gilles Ciment. 2000. "Le Western Selon Gir." In *Trait de Génie: Giraud/Moebius*. CNBDI. http://gciment.free.fr/bdentretiengiraud.htm.

Giraud, Jean, Alain Ledoux, Olivier Maltret, and Gilles Ratier. 1993. "Giraud & Moebius." *Sapristi!*, November 1993.

Giraud, Jean, and Claude Moliterni. 1970. "Gir." *Phénix*, 4e trimestre 1970.

Giraud, Jean, and Numa Sadoul. 1974. "Entretien Avec Jean Giraud." *Schtroumpf: Les Cahiers de La Bande Dessinée*, July 1974.

Giraud, Jean, and Numa Sadoul. 2021. *Docteur Moebius et mister Gir: Entretiens avec Jean Giraud*. Bruxelles, Paris: Casterman.

Giraud, Jean, and Kim Thompson. 1987. "The Other Side of Moebius: An Interview with Jean Giraud." *The Comics Journal*, December 1987.

Glénat-Guttin, Jacques. 1971. "La Gazette de La Bande Dessinée." *Charlie Mensuel*, 4th trimester, 1971.

Gombrich, Ernst. 1968. "Style." In *International Encyclopedia of the Social Sciences*, 15:352–61. https://monoskop.org/File:Gombrich_Ernst_1968_2009_Style.pdf.

Gombrich, Ernst. 1996. "Psychology and the Riddle of Style." In *The Essential Gombrich*, 83–111. London: Phaidon.

Groensteen, Thierry. 2006. *La Bande Dessinée: Un Objet Culturel Non Identifié*. Essais. Angoulême: An 2.

Groensteen, Thierry. 2007. *The System of Comics*. Translated by Nick Nguyen and Bart Beaty. Jackson: University Press of Mississippi.

Groensteen, Thierry. 2012. "Style." *Neuvième Art* 2.0, October 2012. http://neuviemeart.citebd.org/spip.php?article464.

Groensteen, Thierry. 2016. "La fabrique de la bande dessinée." *Genesis: Manuscrits – Recherche – Invention* 43 (December): 43–50. https://doi.org/10.4000/genesis.1702.

Groensteen, Thierry, and Gilles Ciment. 2000. *Trait de génie: Giraud-Moebius*. Angoulême: Centre national de la Bande dessinée et de l'image.

Groensteen, Thierry, and Ann Miller. 2017. *The Expanding Art of Comics: Ten Modern Masterpieces*. Jackson: University Press of Mississippi.

Hajdu, David. 2008. *The Ten-Cent Plague: The Great Comic-Book Scare and How It Changed America*. 1st ed. New York: Farrar, Straus and Giroux.

Hatfield, Charles. 2005. *Alternative Comics: An Emerging Literature*. Jackson: University Press of Mississippi.

Hatfield, Charles. 2012. *Hand of Fire: The Comics Art of Jack Kirby*. Great Comics Artists Series. Jackson: University Press of Mississippi.

Heikkilä, Melissa. 2022. "This Artist Is Dominating AI-Generated Art. And He's Not Happy about It." *MIT Technology Review*, September 16, 2022. https://www.technologyreview.com/2022/09/16/1059598/this-artist-is-dominating-ai-generated-art-and-hes-not-happy-about-it/.

Kelly, Sean. 2015. "Re: A Book on Heavy Metal," December 8, 2015.

Kidman, Shawna. 2019. *Comic Books Incorporated: How the Business of Comics Became the Business of Hollywood*. Oakland: University of California Press.

Knight, Will. 2022. "Algorithms Can Now Mimic Any Artist. Some Artists Hate It." *Wired*, August 19, 2022. https://www.wired.com/story/artists-rage-against-machines-that-mimic-their-work/.

Kohn, Jessica. 2018. "'Travailler Dans Les Petits Mickeys': Les Dessinateurs-Illustrateurs En France et En Belgique de 1945 à 1968." Phd diss., Sorbonne Paris Cité. http://www.theses.fr/2018USPCA024.

Kohn, Jessica. 2021. "Approche Bédéphile Ou Approche Professionnelle: Comment Définir Le Métier de Dessinateur de Bande Dessinée ?" *Comicalités*, April. https://doi.org/10.4000/comicalites.6203.

Kurtzman, Harvey, Sylvie Brod, and Jacques Bisceglia. 1988. "Harvey Kurtzman." *Le Collectionneur de Bandes Dessinées*, printemps 1988.

Labarre, Nicolas. 2014. "Joining the Fray?: *Mad* on Richard Nixon and Spiro Agnew." *Studies in American Humor* 30: 135–54.

Labarre, Nicolas. 2017. *Heavy Metal*, l'autre *Métal Hurlant*. SF Incognita. Bordeaux: Presses Universitaire de Bordeaux.

Labarre, Nicolas. 2018. "Absent Humanity: Personification and Spatialization in 'There Will Come Soft Rains.'" In *Comics and Adaptation*, edited by Benoît Mitaine, David Roche, Isabelle Schmitt-Pitiot, Aarnoud Rommens, and Benoît Mitaine, 66–83. Jackson: University Press of Mississippi.

Labarre, Nicolas. 2020. "'The Illustrated Fantasy Magazine from France.' From Métal Hurlant to Heavy Metal." *Journal of Comics and Culture* 5: 111–30.

Labarre, Nicolas. 2022a. "Moebius [Jean Giraud] (1938–2012)." https://hal.science/hal-03608878.

Labarre, Nicolas. 2022b. "Giraud/Moebius: Redessiner." Billet. *Picturing It!* (blog). March 8, 2022. https://picturing.hypotheses.org/1129.

Lecigne, Bruno, and Jean-Pierre Tamine. 2014. "Modern Realism." In *The French Comics Theory Reader*, edited by Ann Miller and Bart Beaty, 209–24. Leuven: Leuven University Press.

Lefèvre-Vakana, Philippe. 2011. "A La Recherche d'un Chef-d'œuvre de Raymond Poïvet." *Neuvième Art* 2.0. http://neuviemeart.citebd.org/spip.php?article437.

Legoux. 2008. "Le Chasseur Déprime." *Du9*, December. https://www.du9.org/chronique/chasseur-deprime-le/.

Lesage, Sylvain. 2014. "L'effet Codex, Quand La Bande Dessinée Gagne Le Livre: L'album de Bande Dessinée En France de 1950 à 1990." PhD diss., Université Versailles Saint Quentin.

Lesage, Sylvain. 2019a. *L'effet livre: Métamorphoses de la bande dessinée*. Iconotextes. Tours: Presses Universitaire François Rabelais.

Lesage, Sylvain. 2019b. "Une bande dessinée adulte?: Usages et mésusages de la légitimation." *Belphégor: Littérature populaire et culture médiatique* 17 (March). https://doi.org/10.4000/belphegor.1607.

Lesage, Sylvain. 2022. *Ninth Art. Bande Dessinée, Books and the Gentrification of Mass Culture, 1964–1975*. S.l.: Palgrave Macmillan.

Levin, Bob. 2003. *The Pirates and the Mouse: Disney's War against the Counter Culture*. Seattle: Fantagraphics.

Marmonnier, Christian, and Gilles Poussin. 2005. *Métal Hurlant 1975–1987: La Machine à Rêver*. Paris: Denoël.

McIntree, David. 2005. *Beautiful Monsters: The Unofficial and Unauthorized Guide to the Alien and Predator Movies*. 1st edition. Candor, NY: Telos.

McNeil, Carla Speed. 2017. "Foundational Comics." *Carla Speed McNeil* (blog). March 21, 2017. http://www.carlaspeedmcneil.com/blog/2017/3/21/foundational-comics.

Mercier, Jean-Pierre, and Nicolas Labarre. 2022. "'Et zut pour ces quelques fleurs!': Entretien avec Jean-Pierre Mercier sur la bédéphilie." *Comicalités. Études de culture graphique*, February. https://doi.org/10.4000/comicalites.6806.

Mézières, Jean-Claude, and Gary Groth. 2004. "Recognition: A Conversation with Jean-Claude Mézières." *The Comics Journal*, June 2004. https://www.tcj.com/recognition-a-conversation-with-jean-claude-mezieres/.

Michallat, Wendy. 2018. *French Cartoon Art in the 1960s and 1970s: Pilote Hebdomadaire and the Teenager Bande Dessinée*: Studies in European Comics and Graphic Novels. Leuven: Leuven University Press.

Michaut, Xavier. 2019. "Exposition Miyazaki-Moebius." *Buta Connection*. https://www.buta-connection.net/index.php/fans/evenements/exposition-miyazaki-moebius?start=2.

Minne, Samuel. 2012. "Notes sur la science-fiction de Mœbius." Billet. *ReS Futurae* (blog). March 17, 2012. https://resf.hypotheses.org/570.

Moebius. 1975. "Editorial 1." *Métal Hurlant*, 4th trimester, 1975.

Moebius. 1980. *Major Fatal*. Moebius Oeuvres Complètes 3. Paris: Les Humanoïdes Associés.

Moebius. 1981. "Avant-propos." In *Œuvres complètes tome 3: Major Fatal*, 7–9. Paris: Les Humanoïdes Associés.

Moebius. 1984. *Venise Céleste*. Collection Trajets, vol. 1. Paris: Ædena.

Moebius. 1987a. "Afterword to 'Aedena.'" In *Upon a Star*, n.p. Moebius: The Collected Fantaisies of Jean Giraud 1. New York: Epic/Marvel.

Moebius. 1987b. "Afterword to 'The Long Tomorrow.'" In *The Long Tomorrow & Other Science Fiction Stories*, n.p. [23]. Moebius. The Collected Fantasies of Jean Giraud. 3. New York: Epic/Marvel.

Moebius. 1990. "Afterword to 'The Horny Goof.'" In *Moebius 0. The Forbidden Work of Jean Giraud*, n.p. [53]. Milwaukee: Dark Horse.

Moebius. 1999. *Moebius-Giraud, Histoire de Mon Double*. Paris: Editions 1.

Moebius. 2010. "Arzak." In *Arzak l'Arpenteur*, 67–68. Grenoble, Paris: Glénat & Moebius Production.

Moebius. 2011. *Le garage hermétique*. Paris: Les Humanoïdes associés.

Moebius, and Jean-Marc Vidal. 1999. "L'éternel Retour de Moebius." *BoDoï*, June 1999.

"Mœbius-Transe-Forme." 2010. Fondation Cartier Pour l'art Contemporain. 2010. https://www.fondationcartier.com/en/exhibitions/mbius-transe-forme.

Moliterni, Claude, and Gérard Guégan. 1972. *1er Congrès International de la B.D. à New York-Avril 1972*. 16 mm—Noir et Blanc. Reportage—Documentaire. S.F.B.D. Paris—Ministère de l'Éducation nationale et de la Recherche. http://bdzoom.com/5315/patrimoine/1%C2%Bocongres-de-la-bande-dessinee-a-new-york/.

Mollier. 1999. "Aux Origines de La Loi Du 16 Juillet 1949, La Croisade de l'abbé Bethléem Contre Les Illustrés Étrangers." In *On Tue à Chaque Page!: La Loi de 1949 Sur Les Publications Destinées à La Jeunesse*, edited by Thierry Crepin and Thierry Groensteen, 17–34. Paris : [Angoulême]: Éd. du Temps Musée de la bande dessinée.

Molotiu, Andrei. 2020. "Cartooning." In *Comics Studies: A Guidebook*, edited by Charles Hatfield and Bart Beaty, 153–71. New Brunswick, NJ: Rutgers University Press.

Mulatier, Jean. 1975. “Rien Que Du Dessin.” *Mormoil*, September 1975.

O’Bannon, Dan, Ron Cobb, and Dennis Fischer. 1979. “Designing Alien Cultures: Interviews with Dan O’Bannon & Ron Cobb.” *Rocket Blast*, April 1979.

Olzendiel, Ruth, and Karin Zachmann. 2009. “Kitchens as Technology and Politics: An Introduction.” In *Cold War Kitchen: Americanization, Technology and European Users*, 1–29. Cambridge, MA: MIT Press.

Ory, Pascal. 2002. *Le petit nazi illustré: Vie et survie du Téméraire (1943–1944)*. 2nd ed. augmentée. Paris: Nautilus.

Ory, Pascal. 2007. *Goscinny, 1926–1977: La Liberté d’en Rire*. Paris: Perrin.

Pasamonik, Didier. 2013. “Métal Hurlant & (A Suivre), Les Révolutionnaires de La Bande Dessinée s’exposent à Landerneau.” Actua BD: L’actualité de La Bande Dessinée. December 18, 2013. http://www.actuabd.com/Metal-Hurlant-A-Suivre-les.

Pavich, Frank. 2013. *Jodorowsky’s Dune*. Documentaire. Highline Pictures, Camera One, Endless Picnic.

Peltz, Jonathan. 2021. “On ‘Sable’: ‘You’ll See Other Quests in the Game That Are a Bit Silly.’” *Wired*, September 22, 2021. https://www.wired.com/story/sable-game-interview-shedworks-creative-director/.

Pizzoli, Daniel. 1995. *Il était une fois Blueberry: Charlier, Giraud*. Paris Barcelone Bruxelles [etc.]: Dargaud.

Pizzoli, Daniel. 2013. *Moebius, Ou, Les Errances Du Trait*. Mémoire Vive. Montrouge: PLG.

Pizzoli, Daniel. 2021. “La face cachée de Gir.” In *Moebius métamorphe*, 15–24. Paris: Les Humanoïdes associés.

Postema, Barbara. 2013. *Narrative Structure in Comics: Making Sense of Fragments*. Rochester: RIT.

Ratier, Gilles. 1988. “1959–1972 ‘PILOTE.’” *Hop* 44 (3e trimestre): 21–32.

Ratier, Gilles. 2012. “Pour se souvenir de Jean Giraud (alias Gir ou Moebius). . . .” *BDzoom*, March 27, 2012. http://bdzoom.com/47677/patrimoine/pour-se-souvenir-de-jean-giraud%e2%80%a6/.

Renoux, Jean-Philippe. 1979. “Moebius Ou Les Limbes de l’inconscient.” *PLGPPUR*, printemps-été 1979.

Rhodes, RM. 2012. “Screaming at Heavy Metal.” *The Hooded Utilitarian*, October 29, 2012. http://www.hoodedutilitarian.com/2012/10/screaming-at-heavy-metal/.

Rivière, François. 1974. “Gir Fantastiqueur.” *Schtroumpf: Les Cahiers de La Bande Dessinée*, 2nd semester, 1974.

Roux, Antoine. 1974. “Jean Giraud Ou Une Leçon de Montage.” *Schtroumpf, Les Cahiers de La Bande Dessinée*, 2nd semester, 1974.

Sattouf, Riad. 2020. *Riad Sattouf: 100 dessins pour la liberté de la presse*. L’album RSF pour la liberté de la presse 65. Paris: Reporters sans frontières.

Seneca, Matt. 2018. “Moebius’s Last: Le Maître à La Fin.” *The Comics Journal*, October 23, 2018. https://www.tcj.com/moebiuss-last-le-maitre-a-la-fin/.

Sfar, Joann. 2012. Twitter. March 10, 2012. https://twitter.com/joannsfar/status/178505440009793536.

Sfar, Joann, and Jean-Laurent Truc. 2019. "Interview Joann Sfar : « Écrire Blueberry a été difficile »." *Ligne Claire*, November 15, 2019. https://www.ligneclaire.info/blueberry-amertume-apache-92588.html.

Singh, Mahendra. 2012a. "Moebius & The Airtight Garage: No. 2 . . . on a Clear-Line Day, You Can See Forever." *The Hunting of the Snark* (blog). April 2, 2012. https://justtheplaceforasnark.blogspot.com/2012/04/moebius-airtight-garage-no-2-on-clear.html.

Singh, Mahendra. 2012b. "Moebius & The Airtight Garage: No. 3 . . . I Ink the Body Electric." *The Hunting of the Snark* (blog). April 9, 2012. https://justtheplaceforasnark.blogspot.com/2012/04/moebius-airtight-garage-no-3-i-ink-body.html.

Smolderen, Thierry. 1984. "Jean Gir, Le Nouveau Moebius." *Les Cahiers de La Bande Dessinée*, July 1984.

Smolderen, Thierry. 2000. "La galaxie Moebius." *Neuvième art* 2.0. http://neuviemeart.citebd.org/spip.php?article378.

Smolderen, Thierry. 2014. *The Origins of Comics: From William Hogarth to Winsor McCay*. Jackson: University Press of Mississippi.

Sternberg, Jacques, Michel Caen, and Jacques Lob, eds. 1967. *Les Chefs-d'œuvre de la bande dessinée*. Paris, France: Éditions Planète.

Suzuki, Shige (CJ). 2022. "Katsuhiro Ōtomo." In *Fifty Key Figures in Cyberpunk Culture*, edited by Anna McFarlane, Graham J. Murphy, and Lars Schmeink, 143–48. New York: Routledge, Taylor & Francis.

Talibon-Lapomme, Edward. 1970. "Du Nouveau . . . à l'ouest." *Combat*, June 17, 1970.

Tellier, Maxime. 2021. "France-Soir: Grandeur et déliquescence d'un journal devenu anti-journalistique." *France Culture*, March 14, 2021. https://www.radiofrance.fr/franceculture/france-soir-grandeur-et-deliquescence-d-un-journal-devenu-anti-journalistique-9661755.

Thompson, Kim. 1982. "Keeping Up with Moebius." *The Comics Journal*, May 1982.

Thompson, Kim. 2012. "Jean 'Moebius' Giraud, 1938–2012." *The Comics Journal*, March 12, 2012. https://www.tcj.com/jean-moebius-giraud-1938-2012/.

Tomblaine, Philippe. 2019. "Le retour de Blueberry: Antihéros amér(icain) selon Sfar et Blain." *BDzoom*, November 25, 2019. http://bdzoom.com/148966/lart-de/le-retour-de-blueberry-antiheros-americain-selon-sfar-et-blain/.

Trondheim, Lewis. 2005. *Désoeuvré*. Eprouvette: L'Association.

Trondheim, Lewis, and Jean Giraud. 1996. "Moebius-Trondheim: Discution à Double Sens Unique." *Le Lézard*, January 1996.

Valembois, Diane. 2004. *Miyazaki, Moebius: 2 artistes dont les dessins prennent vie: exposition du 1er décembre 2004 au 13 mars 2005, Musée de la Monnaie de Paris*. Paris: BVI-France. http://catalogue.bnf.fr/ark:/12148/cb400140010.

Webster, Andrew. 2018. "Sable Looks like a Moebius Comic and Plays like Breath of the Wild." *The Verge*, June 14, 2018. https://www.theverge.com/2018/6/14/17462494/sable-xbox-preview-moebius-zelda-e3-2018.

Wiater, Stanley, and Stephen R. Bissette. 1993. *Comic Book Rebels: Conversations with the Creators of the New Comics*. New York: Donald I. Fine.

Williams, Paul. 2020. *Dreaming the Graphic Novel: The Novelization of Comics*. New Brunswick: Rutgers University Press.

Wivel, Matthias. 2009. "The Constant Garage." *The Comics Journal*, November 2009.

Wivel, Matthias. 2012. "Chasseur Déprime." *The Hooded Utilitarian* (blog). March 13, 2012. https://www.hoodedutilitarian.com/tag/chasseur-deprime/.

INDEX

ABOUT THE AUTHOR

Photo by Claude Labarre

Nicolas Labarre is professor of American studies at University Bordeaux Montaigne, France, where he teaches about US political institutions, comics, and videogames. He is author of *Heavy Metal, l'autre "Métal Hurlant"* (2017), a transnational history of *Heavy Metal* magazine, and of *Understanding Genres in Comics* (2020).